LAW FORUM SERIES

College of Law, Ohio State University

THE NEGRO AND
THE FIRST AMENDMENT

The Negro and the First Amendment

by
HARRY KALVEN, JR.

Ohio State University Press
Columbus
1965

Preface

THESE LECTURES were originally given for the Ohio State Law Forum on April 7, 8, and 9, 1964. After due reflection, I have decided to leave them, except for some editorial changes, in the form in which they were given. The momentum of the lecture format seems to me congenial to my thesis.

The Negro civil rights movement bids fair to be the most fully documented revolution in history. This is one more book about the movement, and some apologia for it may be appropriate.

The concern of this book is a special one: it is with the impact of a massive political and social phenomenon on the law, especially constitutional law. What novelty there is in the approach is perhaps suggested by the title. The focus is not on the major developments that have taken place within this generation in giving the Negro his due, his constitutional due, under the Fourteenth Amendment. The focus is rather on a less noticed aspect of the constitutional revolution—the impact of the civil rights movement on the First Amendment.

The result is a book which is at once about
the Negro movement and about First Amendment
theory. The story is, I think, a happy and encour-
aging one. The extraordinary tact and sure instinct
of the Negro protest has made it primarily a massive petition for the redress of grievances, a form
of political action, in the courts and in the streets.
And a gallant and sensitive United States Supreme
Court has responded. Further, and this is the special
point, the Court has responded *as a court* and has
found the rationale for its decisions in an appropriate and exciting reworking of First Amendment
doctrine.

That the lectures were given six months ago
poses certain problems. This is an area of law and
political action subject to very rapid changes. I
have, however, decided not to update the manuscript.
It speaks as of April, 1964. The Negro movement
has, despite dire predictions, survived the "long hot
summer" of 1964 with no basic changes; it con-
tinues, whatever the sporadic outbreaks of violence,
to show grace, courage, and patience.

A note has been added to the third lecture, in
order to look briefly at the civil rights legislation
of 1964 and the June 22, 1964, decisions of the
Court in the latest series of sit-in cases. Also, notes
have been added to cover two other relevant decisions of the Court which have come down since the
date of the lectures.

Finally, there is a special awkwardness with respect to the first lecture. I have, in the intervening months, had the opportunity to write further on the *New York Times* case and the significance of seditious libel.* The two treatments are complementary, but there is inevitably some overlapping, and possibly some difference in emphasis.

I am indebted to Alexander Meiklejohn, Robert Hutchins, Frank Strong, Philip Kurland, and Kenneth Karst, all of whom were kind enough to read over the manuscript. I owe a considerable debt to Mr. Hutchins and the Center for the Study of Democratic Institutions for the opportunity to spend the summer of 1963 at the Center. The materials in the third lecture in particular reflect the stimulus of this visit.

Finally, I am deeply grateful to Dean Strong and his faculty for their warm hospitality and enthusiasm.

HARRY KALVEN, JR.

Chicago
September, 1964

* Kalven, *The New York Times Case—A Note on the Central Meaning of the First Amendment,* [1964] SUP.CT REV. 191

Contents

THE NEGRO AND
THE FIRST AMENDMENT

Introduction

THE UNIFYING THEME for these three lectures may not be quite self-evident. The greatest fascination of law study is, I think, to watch some great event from the real world intersect with existing legal doctrine. This is especially so in constitutional law because, as De Toqueville first noted, in America, with judicial review, all great issues of public policy become justiciable. Certainly the great event on the domestic scene in recent years has been the emergence of the Negro rights protest movment, and certainly this remarkable social and political phenomenon is having its repercussions on constitutional law. In general, I shall assume these are familiar. They center, as they should, on the meaning and reach of the Fourteenth Amendment as a source of *federal* power. The accelerated evolution of legal doctrine here during my own professional lifetime has been truly remarkable. It has been a great achievement of democratic law—although we have all had to make our peace with Professor

Wechsler's challenge as to whether the great cases, *Smith* v. *Allwright*,[1] *Shelley* v. *Kraemer*,[2] and *Brown* v. *Board of Education*,[3] can be clothed in neutral principle.[4] It is my special purpose, however, to by-pass these important constitutional themes and to look at the impact of the Negro issue on another corner of the constitutional fabric: that of free speech. To join two popular labels of the day, it is an effort, if you will, to trace connections between civil rights and civil liberties. You may suspect, and you would not be entirely wrong to do so, that this unifying theme of the Negro and the First Amendment is something of a trick, a way of infusing an old topic with the glamor and excitement of the day's headlines. But the point is more than rhetorical. Surely so major a social phenomenon must put new questions to our doctrines of speech and association. We hear talk of the "Negro Revolution" or even of the "Second American Revolution";[5] the Negro is testing today not only our good will and decency but also our processes for orderly and peaceful revolution.

I have one further prefatory obligation to discharge. My inquiry is into the impact of the Negro issue on free-speech theory. It presupposes agreement that the quest for coherent general theory in matters of the First Amendment needs no apology and no defense. Yet there is a puzzle here. In general, the law has a great capacity to tolerate inconsistencies; perhaps the most difficult thing for

the beginning law student to grasp is this sense of
tolerable inconsistency. Robert Merton has said
that in its present state sociology could aspire only
to theories "in the middle range"; in law, we aim
less high. To take a page from torts for the
moment, if I were to say that my purpose was to
struggle with a liability theory that has one basis
of liability for industrial accidents and another for
non-industrial accidents,[6] or that has one basis for
liability in defamation and another for physical
harms,[7] you would think I was a purist with unreasonable expectations of generality. When, however, it is, as it will be, a question of fitting control
of defamation or obscenity or contempt of court
into free-speech notions, we accept the challenge
as proper.

The "feel" is different. When some fifteen years
ago Alexander Meiklejohn published his book *Free
Speech and Its Relation to Self-Government,*[8] there
was uniform appreciation of his desire to find a
unifying theory for the First Amendment whatever the reactions to the particular theory he put
forth. We did not say that as a non-lawyer he was
confusing philosophy with law. And only a year
ago, so seasoned a law professional as Professor
Emerson of Yale published a lengthy article under
the title "Toward a General Theory of the First
Amendment," which began with a complaint that we
had "no really adequate or comprehensive theory of
the First Amendment."[9]

I leave you to brood about the law's appetite for

theory. If my puzzle as to the First Amendment is not a true puzzle, it can only be for the congenial reason that free speech is so close to the heart of democratic organization that if we do not have an appropriate theory for our law here, we feel we really do not understand the society in which we live.

In any event, in these lectures I will accept the obligations of theory. I propose to examine in some detail three fresh problems for free-speech theory churned up by the Negro issue:

1. The problem of group defamation, especially as illumined by *Beauharnais* v. *Illinois*,[10] decided in 1952, and with a nod to *Sullivan* v. *New York Times*,[11] decided only last month.

2. The problems created by legal efforts to curb and control the NAACP. Here the key case will be *Gibson* v. *Florida Legislative Investigation Committee*,[12] decided in 1963.

3. The problems of Negro self-help tactics and the extent to which they can be regarded as a new form of speech entitled to certain privileges. Here the key case is *Garner* v. *Louisiana*,[13] decided in 1961, unless while we are meeting here the Court should hand down its decision in the sit-in cases.[14]

To anticipate what may emerge as a final conclusion, and as a thumbnail summary of the last two or three decades of speech issues in the Supreme Court, we may come to see the Negro as winning back for us the freedoms the Communists seemed to have lost for us.

I

Group Libel, Seditious Libel, and Just Plain Libel

IT IS STRANGE how rapidly things change. Just a little more than a decade ago we were all concerned with devising legal controls for the libeling of groups. The war and the rise of fascism had made us suddenly sensitive to the evils of systematic defamation of minority groups, sensitive to the new and unexpected power of malevolent propaganda. Existing doctrines of free speech appeared to cast long shadows over the validity of any legal efforts at control. Then, in 1952, the Supreme Court got its chance at the problem and in *Beauharnais* v. *Illinois*[15] held that group-libel laws could be constitutional.

Ironically, once the victory was won, the momentum for such legal measures seemed to dissipate, and the problem has all but disappeared from view. It is instructive to note, for example, that Illinois, when it revised its criminal code in 1961, withdrew from it the very statute the Court had ratified in the Beauharnais case.[16] It is probable that among today's law students few have been called upon to think about group libel and that a fair number have never heard the term.

The story is thus not a long one and seems to have come to a tranquil ending. Yet I would like to retell it in some detail. In many ways I find *Beauharnais* v. *Illinois* the precedent on free speech most worthy of close study; and I find the various opinions of the Court the most telltale evidence that we do not have an acceptable theory and doctrine of the First Amendment. And, as you doubtless know, the topic has been given a last-minute bonus of excitement and currency by the Court's recent decision in the *New York Times* case.[17]

It is important at the outset to isolate just what behavior group libel refers to.[18] The Nazi success in exploiting anti-Semitism provided the model of a new virulent form of defamation. It was systematic; it was a deliberate tactic; it was aimed at vulnerable minorities, not individuals; it was designed to foment hatred and strife. To use a contemporary adjective, it was "sick." Indeed, the alerting of law to this new form of malevolent behavior can be viewed as one of sociology's more immediate contributions to law. It is no accident that the major article on it came in 1942 from David Riesman, then still a professor of law but clearly already en route to his distinguished career as a social scientist.

Let me quote a few sentences from the Riesman article, which bore the striking title, "Democracy and Defamation: The Control of Group Libel":

> The samples . . . are not the daily grist of vituperative political debate. Nor do they represent the frothy imaginings of lunatics, or the idle gossip of a country town. Rather they indicate the systematic avalanche of falsehoods which are circulated concerning the various groups, classes, and races, which make up the countries of the western world. . . . Such purposeful attacks are nothing new, of course. . . . What is new, however, is the existence of a mobile public opinion as the controlling force in politics and the systematic manipulation of that opinion by the use of calculated falsehood and vilification. . . . Obviously, therefore, defamation and the law of defamation have become weapons in the political struggle between democracy and fascism.[19]

The image was that of a kind of hard-core libel, analogous in offensiveness to hard-core pornography.[20] The Indiana legislature, for example, in passing a special statute to meet the problem used the phrase "hate racketeering."[21]

The definitive profile of the evil, however, comes from the great pen of Justice Jackson, back from the Nuremberg trials and dissenting in 1951 in the case of *Kunz* v. *New York,* which involved the licensing of a fascist-like speech in the public parks:[22]

Equally inciting and more clearly "fighting words" when thrown at Catholics and Jews, who are rightfully on the streets of New York, are statements that "The Pope is the anti-Christ" and the Jews are "Christ-killers." These terse epithets come down to our generation weighted with hatreds accumulated through centuries of bloodshed. They are recognized words of art in the profession of defamation. They are not the kind of insult that men bandy and laugh off when the spirits are high and the flagons are low. They are not in that class of epithets whose literal sting will be drawn if the speaker smiles when he uses them. They are always and in every context insults which do not spring from reason and can be answered by none. Their historical associations with violence are well understood both by those who hurl and those who are struck by these missiles. Jews, many of whose families perished in extermination furnaces in Dachau and Auschwitz, are more than tolerant if they pass off lightly the suggestion that nonbelievers in Christ should all have been burned.

How does this concern with dramatic group defamation connect up with the Negro? The Beauharnais case did in fact involve anti-Negro propaganda, so we can claim a sufficient connection for the purposes at hand. And proposals for group-libel legislation are invariably keyed to "racial, religious, or national groups" and would include protection of Negroes. But beyond this lies an intriguing sociological puzzle. The Negro protest, which has proceeded on a very wide legal and self-help front, has not sought to utilize the particular legal weapon of group-libel law. In this respect there has been a striking contrast between the Negro and Jewish response to prejudice.[23] The Jewish groups have been extremely sensitive to defamation and extremely alert to combat it at every turn. A major Jewish organization is called the Anti-Defamation League. The Negro, even now, at the height of sensitivity to his rights, seems indifferent to defamation.

Tracing why this is so would, I think, provide an engaging point for attitude research; at the moment conjecture will have to suffice. Perhaps it is simply a reflection of the uniquely terrible Jewish experience in Nazi Germany. Perhaps there is less white supremacy *talk* than there is anti-Semitic talk. Perhaps the sensitivity to verbal assault is different for the Negro and for the Jewish cultures. Perhaps it is an indication of how much deeper the Negro grievance really is. Anti-Semitism may be the artifact of myth and the cumulative defamation of centuries; race prejudice in the United States today stems, I suspect, from the brutal and objectively real heritage of slavery. One is tempted to say that it will be a sign that the Negro problem has basically been solved when the Negro begins to worry about group-libel protection. In any event, it is striking that no one urges today, amidst the plethora of proposals for producing racial tolerance, that we must protect the reputation of the Negroes as a group; and it is a sign of the strategy by which I have imposed unity on my three lectures that the chief point to make about the Negro and group-libel law is that the Negro does not seek to use it!

This then was the evil of group libel, and it was real. We need to put a few additional facts into place to set properly the backdrop for the Beau- harnais case. First there is a chapter of constitu- tional evolution, which I can assume is reasonably familiar: the rise of the clear and present danger test as the measure of permissible government inter- ference with speech.[24] The actual evolution of the test is a complex story in its own right. And there are commentators, like Professor Emerson, who think that by and large the test has been aban- doned by the court today.[25] It is certainly true that its beginnings in *Schenck*[26] were quite different from what it was finally said to have become, and quite different from what Brandeis was able to make of it in *Whitney*.[27] It is true that it is a legal test which has always had far greater status in non-law circles than in the legal world. It may be true that there is no speech case in which a defend- ant wins because of the bite of the test. It is true that the test is rich in ambiguity, that some of the Court, and particularly Justice Frankfurter,[28] have never admitted it was more than a felicitous phrase.

Indeed it may be a prime example, along with *res ipsa loquitur* and last clear chance, of the capacity of a striking phrase to capture the legal mind and to turn itself into doctrine.[29] In general, praised as the measure of our great love of liberty, it has been criticized by Alexander Meiklejohn for its abject surrender of freedom of spech.[30] And in the Dennis case in 1951, it was restated by Judge Learned Hand as something analogous to the calculus of risk in negligence so that the gravity of the danger is discounted by its proximity; with the result that if the danger is great enough, it need not be present before government can act.[31] Finally the Dennis case at the level of the Supreme Court—although the Court ratified the Hand revision of the formula—can be read as a definitive showing of the strength of the test and of the almost uncanny power of the dissents of Holmes and Brandeis.[32] By the end of 1951, while a few close students of the speech cases might wonder if the famed test was not a myth unrelated to any actual pattern of decisions, it loomed large in the idiom of judicial opinion and was, in effect, the handle by which the Court would be expected to pick up a speech problem.

This brief glance at the clear and present danger formula is relevant to our immediate purposes because of a special characteristic of the evil of group defamation which we have yet to note. Systematic group libel, although a very nasty business, does not normally carry a clear and present danger of anything; unlike other troublesome speech, it does not advocate or incite, its words are not "triggers of action." Its evils are slower, and corrosive. Once again we are reminded of obscenity. This absence of a specific danger from group libel, the proximity of which could be measured, was often noted by commentators, even as they described its special evils.

Thus Francis Biddle, speaking as attorney-general of the United States at a Law School Association symposium during the war, stated:

> Now the anti-Semitic propaganda on which I have touched doesn't incite to violence; it is not seditious; it certainly gives rise to no clear and present danger, but it is full of lies and it borders continually on the libellous, on the group libellous.[33]

And a *Columbia Law Review* note writer, proposing a group-libel statute in 1947, tells us:

> The most dangerous libel is defamatory propaganda that does not necessarily incite to immediate breaches of the peace, but nevertheless is mendacious, threatens minority groups and endangers ultimately democratic society itself.[34]

While, as the quotation from Justice Jackson has so vividly suggested, the terse historic epithets of group defamation may move the vulnerable audience to strike back at the speaker, such outbursts of violence are not the necessary consequence of such speech and, more important, such violence when it does occur is not the serious evil of the speech.

We now have three of our needed ingredients: the new and serious evils of this special form of malevolence, the salience of the clear and present danger test as the measure of the First Amendment, and the perception that, whatever its evil, group defamation does not readily present anything that can be called a clear and present danger. We are still missing one final factor—the nature and significance of seditious libel.

Seditious libel is the doctrine that flourished in England during and after the ascendancy of the Star Chamber.[35] In brief, it is the doctrine that criticism of government officials and policy may be viewed as defamation of government and may be punished as a serious crime. Although it is a term of art from English law, it is found as the hallmark of all closed societies throughout the world. It makes an important chapter in English history, legal and constitutional, and it has its special heroes, its Erskine and its Fox. The treatment of such speech as criminal is based on an accurate perception of the dangers in it; it is likely to undermine confidence in government policy and in the official incumbents. But it is a profound tenet of democracy that no government official has the legal power to silence such commentary about himself.

I have now, perhaps, reached the point where I can let my pet cat out of the bag. On my view, the absence of seditious libel as a crime is the true pragmatic test of freedom of speech. This I would argue is what freedom of speech is about. Any society in which seditious libel is a crime is, no matter what its other features, not a free society. A society can, for example, either treat obscenity as a crime or not treat it as a crime without thereby altering its basic nature as a society. It seems to me it cannot do so with seditious libel. Here the response to this crime defines the society.

I have talked rather loosely thus far of silencing criticism of government policy. As a technical matter, however, what is striking is that the application of the conceptual frame of the law of defamation to government and government officials literally equates with seditious libel.[36] A free society is one in which you cannot defame the government.

If you look closely at the history of free-speech doctrine in the United States, you become conscious of certain critical moments. For example, if Judge Learned Hand's great opinion in the district court in the Masses[37] case in 1917 had not been obliterated by the Schenck opinion in the Supreme Court the same year, the analytic foundations of free speech would have been sounder. The results might well have been much the same, but the doctrine in terms of an "advocacy test" would, I think, have been more lawyer-like. That, however, is a digression. More to the present point is the curious fact that the very concept of seditious libel drops out of our doctrine.[38] The Supreme Court, perhaps because speech has even in its worst days been extraordinarily free in the United States, has—at least not until March, 1964—never been confronted squarely with the problem of seditious libel. The result is that our theory has been encased in the intellectual poverty of the clear and present danger formula; it would for all purposes have been a better theory had it been built around seditious libel as the key concept.

Our history has been odd indeed. We did as a nation have one experience with seditious libel— the Sedition Act of 1798. Listen carefully to its terms:[39]

> . . . If any person shall write print utter or publish . . . any false scandalous and malicious writings against the government of the United States or either house of the Congress of the United States or the President of the United States with intent to defame the said government, or either house of the said Congress, or the said President or to bring them or either of them into contempt, or disrepute; or to excite against them or either or any of them the hatred of the good people of the United States . . . then such person being convicted shall be punished by a fine not exceeding $2,000 and by imprisonment not exceeding two years.

The Act is thus a perfect expression of the doctrine of seditious libel. But the subsequent history
is for present purposes frustrating. The Act expired
by its own terms two years after enactment and
was never revived. None of the handful of cases
prosecuted under it left a serious precedent. It
expired in 1800 as Jefferson came to the presidency
after a sharp switch in political power from Feder-
alists to Jeffersonian Democrats. Jefferson pardoned
violators of the Act still in prison, and some years
later Congress repaid the fines. The change in
political fortunes left an impression that the Act
was not only an egregious political error on the
part of John Adams but unconstitutional as well.
This impression became a definitive conclusion via
an offhand dictum uttered by Justice Holmes in the
course of his eloquent dissent in the Abrams case
in 1919. Said Justice Holmes:

> I wholly disagree with the argument of the
> Government that the First Amendment left the
> common law of seditious libel in force. History
> seems to me against the notion. I had conceived
> that the United States through many years had
> shown its repentance for the Sedition Act of 1798
> by repaying the fines that it imposed.[40]

Once again we cannot pursue properly here an
exciting inquiry, an inquiry made, if anything, more
exciting by the comments of the Supreme Court in
the *New York Times* case. It is unclear whether

the Sedition Act was unconstitutional when enacted; and whether it was or not remains perhaps the most relevant free-speech question we can ask. Until early in 1964, the dictum of Justice Holmes was as close as we had come to having the Court pass on the matter. But a few details do deserve our notice. It is striking that as late as 1919 the government would have seriously argued that the Sedition Act was constitutional;[41] it is striking how unpersuasive the Holmes argument is. One can find competent scholars writing just before the burst of speech cases in World War I, men like Corwin,[42] Hall,[43] and Vance[44] who thought the Act had been constitutional, and one can find my colleague William Crosskey[45] and Leonard Levy, in his *Legacy of Suppression,*[46] arguing the same conclusion today. Further, there are some oddities, by now well advertised, in the position of Thomas Jefferson on all this.[47] He was an outspoken critic of the Act but was not unwilling to have prosecutions for seditious libel brought under state law against publishers critical of him. Unfortunately, history does not seem so set against the notion as Justice Holmes' page of history would have had us believe; and in this instance we may prefer the volume of logic. For now, my point is simply how small a role the concept of seditious libel has played in our free-speech theorizing, until just the other day, despite its obvious centrality.

If I may be indulged in one last digression, there is one irresistibly interesting additional item about the reputation of the Sedition Act. Every schoolboy knows that the Sedition Act of 1798 is a dirty word, and many schoolboys know that Fox's Libel Act of 1792 is one of the great landmarks on the road to political liberty. It is instructive to compare them since they both dealt with seditious libel. Fox's Libel Act left the crime intact but made one change in the procedure, it made the question of libel a question for the jury—a change of undeniable importance. Section 3 of the Sedition Act, however, also made libel a question for the jury, *and provided further that truth was a defense*. It is thus unarguable that the hated Sedition Act was a more liberal measure vis à vis speech than the admired Fox's Libel Act!

We are now virtually ready to watch the problem of group libel hit the Supreme Court. The Court had two inconclusive skirmishes with fascist libelers just prior to *Beauharnais* in 1952. In *Terminiello*[48] in 1949, they reviewed the conviction of a virulently anti-Semitic speaker under a breach of peace ordinance. The speech was in a private hall but there was a considerable threat of violence in the crowd outside. The Court reversed the decision for an error in the instructions defining breach of peace as, *inter alia,* "stirring the public to anger, inviting dispute, bringing about a condition of unrest," an error incidentally not complained of by the defendant below. By its approach, the Court turned a heated instance of fascistic libel and name-calling into an abstract discussion of the freedom to invite dispute and added little to the problem at hand. Justice Jackson was moved to a dissent which is as effective as it is indignant. He observes "underneath a little issue of Terminiello and his hundred dollar fine lurk some of the most far reaching constitutional questions that can confront a people who value both liberty and order."[49]

The second case is also oblique for present purposes. In *Kunz*[50] in 1951, a comparable speaker was denied a license to speak in a public park, and the precise issue was the validity of the state's criteria for licensing. The Court reversed Kunz's conviction for speaking without a license and held that the licensing arrangements were invalid because they gave no appropriate guides to the discretion of the administrative official. The fine incidentally was ten dollars, and once again Jackson fired an indignant dissent at the unrealism of the result, a dissent from which we earlier quoted.[51]

Although both cases, then, involved "professional" group libelers, neither decision went squarely to the central question of the power of the state to regulate group libel.

In *Beauharnais* the defendant was convicted and fined two hundred dollars for violating a provision of the Illinois criminal code. The statute read as follows:

> It shall be unlawful for any person . . . to publish, present, or exhibit in any public place in this state any lithograph, moving picture, play, drama or sketch which . . . portrays depravity, criminality, unchastity, or lack of virtue of a class of citizens of any race, color, creed or religion which said publication . . . exposes the citizens of any race, color, creed or religion to contempt, derision, or obloquy, or which is productive of breach of the peace or riots. . . .

The statute was not a response to modern fascism, but had been on the books in Illinois since 1917.[52] Despite its curiously awkward phrasing, several things are clear: (1) it is concerned with groups, with a "class of citizens"; (2) it borrows some of the standard formulae of civil libel, expose to "contempt, derision, or obloquy"; (3) the threat of a breach of peace is disjunctive and not necessary to the crime (it is either exposing to contempt, etc., or being productive of breach of peace); (4) unlike either the modern New Jersey statute designed specially for group libel or the model *Columbia Law Review* draft,[53] both of which are limited to defamation of racial, religious, or ethnic groups, the Illinois statute is difficult to construe on this point—although it talks of "race, color, creed or religion," it seems to cover any "class of citizens"; (5) as perhaps an offset, the statute is limited to statements on "depravity, criminality, unchastity, or lack of virtue"—arguably there may be some defamation not covered by these terms and hence outside the scope of the statute.

The publication of the defendant is also difficult to scan. He was president of an organization called the White Circle League of America; and the publication for distribution of which he was convicted was a leaflet, a portion of which was in the form of a petition to the mayor and city council. There was a bold-face heading: "Preserve and Protect White Neighborhoods! from the constant and continuous invasion, harassment and encroachment by the Negroes." There was a membership blank, and more than half the space was devoted to a call for white volunteers who were reminded, "The first loyalty of every white person is to his race." "We want two million signatures of white men and women." The petition section contains four "whereas" clauses commenting on the threat of Negroes to white neighborhoods, their vulnerability to communism, and the "seething" unrest of the white population. The prayer, however, is obscure; it is to use the police power "to halt the encroachment, harassment and further invasion of white people, their property, neighborhoods and persons by the Negro."

We have accounted thus far for 95 per cent of the wordage on the leaflet; and while eccentric and insistently racist in tone, it is surely innocuous as a matter of law. What turns out to be the fatal passage reads as follows:

> The White Circle League of America is the only articulate white voice in America being raised in protest against Negro aggression and infiltration into all white neighborhoods. The white people of Chicago must take advantage of the opportunity to become united. If persuasion and the need to prevent the white race from being mongrelized by the Negro will not unite us, then the aggressions, rapes, robberies, knives, guns and marijuana of the Negro surely will.

To bring matters a little closer to home for us, it is a fair guess that Mr. Beauharnais was protesting the actual and the feared consequences of the decision of the Court in *Shelley* v. *Kraemer* in 1948 outlawing restrictive covenants, a device on which Chicago had relied heavily to produce segregated neighborhoods.

There is little in the brief opinion of the Illinois Supreme Court affirming the conviction that need detain us.[54] The court does observe that the statute is "a form of criminal libel." Because it appears to think, erroneously, that the United States Supreme Court has already upheld the statute in *Bevins* v. *Prindable*,[55] it says little about the defendant's constitutional challenges. The statute is not too vague, and the "mere reading of the petition" shows, the court says, that it "is liable to cause violence and

disorder between the races. . . . Any ordinary
person could only conclude from the libellous character of the language that a clash and riots would
eventually result between the members of the White
Circle League of America and the Negro race." It
is probable that the Illinois court thinks that clear
and present danger is the relevant test and that the
petition, although distributed and not uttered orally,
shows on its face enough evidence of danger to
satisfy the test. At the trial the defendant had
offered to prove the truth of his statements by
showing that crimes were more frequent in Negro
districts, by citing a specific instance of Negro
violence, and by offering testimony that some real
estate values had gone down. The trial court rejected his proffer of proof on the grounds that it
did not go to the truth of the entire charge. The
Illinois Supreme Court affirms and adds, since truth
is a defense in criminal libel in Illinois only when
there are good motives, "It is hard to see how, with
the libellous publication in evidence, any proof of
good motives or justifiable ends could be intro-
duced." At the trial the defendant had requested
an instruction submitting to the jury the issue of
the clear and present danger of "a serious substantive evil that rises far above public inconvenience,
annoyance or unrest." The wording of the instruction indicates he was relying on language in the
Court's opinion in the Terminiello case. The trial

court refused the instruction. The Illinois Supreme
Court affirmed.

There is one last detail about the trial that carries
ironic historical overtones although the Illinois court
does not discuss it. You will recall it is not so easy
to say with just what Beauharnais is charging
Negroes. Nevertheless, the trial judge takes from
the jury any issue of whether the words used are
defamatory, leaving the jury only the uncontro-
verted fact that the defendant did distribute the
leaflet. And this exactly one hundred and sixty
years after the passage in England of Fox's Libel
Act.

We come then to the case in the United States
Supreme Court. In a five to four decision, the
conviction is affirmed. Justice Frankfurter writes
the opinion for the majority; there are four separate dissents by Reed, Black, Douglas, and Jackson.
The opinions in all occupy some fifty-three pages in
the reports and provide the essential text for this
lecture. Justice Frankfurter's majority, it might be
noted, is made up of Minton, Clark, Vinson, and
Burton. The interplay of the various opinions is
rich and dramatic and a good index of the degree
to which the Court had not, by 1952, evolved a
common approach to, and a common theory about,
freedom of speech.

It is difficult to attempt summary of Justice
Frankfurter's opinion without risking being unfair

to it. For present purposes its key sentence occurs very near the end:

> Libellous utterances not being within the area of constitutionally protected speech, it is unnecessary either for us or the State courts, to consider the issues behind the phrase "clear and present danger."[56]

This striking conclusion is in turn based on *two* prior premises which have been carefully made explicit. The first is that the libel of individuals may be punished as a crime without raising constitutional doubts. In developing this thesis, Justice Frankfurter uses *two* lines of analysis: he documents carefully that it was a common-law crime and is today found on the statute books of all fifty states; *and* he quotes the apparently apt language of *Chaplinsky* v. *New Hampshire*[57] that punishment of certain words—fighting words, the lewd, the obscene, the profane, the libelous—"have never been thought to raise any constitutional problem." The second premise is that application of criminal-libel laws to the libel of groups does not raise essentially different issues. He recognizes that he is taking a step at this point and states clearly: "The precise question before us then is whether the protection of liberty in the Due Process Clause of the Fourteenth Amendment prevents a State from punishing such libels—as criminal libel has been defined, limited and constitutionally recognized

time out of mind—directed at designated collec-
tivities and flagrantly disseminated."[58] He admits
this precise question is not concluded by history
and practice and then states the appropriate test
for resolving it:

> If an utterance directed at an individual may
> be the object of criminal sanctions we cannot deny
> to a state power to punish the same utterance
> directed at a defined group, *unless we can say that
> this is a willful and purposeless restriction unre-
> lated to the peace and well being of the state.*[59]

Since I do not want to come back later to this
part of his opinion, let me pause for a moment
here. To use a test limited to whether legislation
is "a willful and purposeless restriction unrelated
to the well being of the State" may sound like a
caricature of the Frankfurter doctrine of judicial
self-restraint in the exercise of judicial review.
Unless the legislation shows the legislature to have
been stark raving mad in enacting it, it is not the
function of the Court to step in. The Frankfurter
formula here is certainly odd, but I would read
it as an indication of the special subtlety of his
analysis. It is not a general formula, it is simply
the formula for the special matter at hand, which
is almost but not quite foreclosed by the analogy
of individual libel. Since it is not quite foreclosed,
he is willing to test the difference; and this then
is the formula for making the test.

It will come as no surprise that the Illinois law, put to this test, readily passes it. There is a careful review of Illinois history of racial violence, a careful nod to the Riesman stress on the importance of group status for insuring individual status. "This being so, we are precluded from saying that speech concededly punishable when immediately directed at individuals cannot be outlawed if directed at groups with whose position and esteem in society the affiliated individual may be inextricably involved." The opinion is thus in part a sociological commentary on the problems of the Negro.

The main structure of the Frankfurter argument is clear, although there are many rich details we are omitting. There are some kinds of speech issues for which clear and present danger is an inappropriate and irrelevant test. Criminal libel of individuals is one such speech problem, and criminal libel of groups is sufficiently close to individual libel so that criminal libel of groups also does not come within the category of speech problems to be tested by clear and present danger. The argument, it should be noted, is no broader than it has to be. It may be true, as the Dennis case the year before had indicated,[60] that Justice Frankfurter did not accept the idea that the clear and present danger formula had constitutional status for any type of speech problem and was interested in ridding free-speech doctrine of this misconception. In *Beau-*

harnais, however, he was making a far narrower attack.

What then do the four dissenters do with this complex argument? We begin with the dissent of Justice Reed. He argues the single point that the Illinois statute is unconstitutionally vague, and he argues it very well indeed. Since the trial judge took the whole issue of defamation away from the jury, we cannot tell which clause of the statute the defendant offended. Consciously following the much admired lawyer's argument of Chief Justice Hughes in the red flag case of the thirties, *Stromberg* v. *California,*[61] Justice Reed then argues that any clause of the statute might have been involved and that, hence, all clauses must pass constitutional scrutiny. He then focusses on the clause making it unlawful to portray "a lack of virtue of a class of citizens which . . . exposes them to derision or obloquy." He argues that the ambiguity of such words is quite different when they are applied to groups than when applied to individuals and that there is, Justice Frankfurter to the contrary, no clue in Illinois precedent as to what these terms mean.

The majority opinion does not ignore the point that the statute was vague. The Frankfurter answer is brief and relies on the "clarifying construction and fixed usage" these words have been given. It is not profitable, of course, to compare opinions as to whether a law is unconstitutionally vague.[62] It is clear from the Winters[63] case, the Burstyn[64] case, and the Roth[65] case that the court will tolerate enormous ambiguity in terms which have some sort of common-law history behind them and where the community sense of the jury is relied on. Yet here the issue was withdrawn from the jury, and the history and tradition of meaning is in individual libel. Perhaps, in the end, the argument over vagueness simply highlights the difficulties in moving as easily as Justice Frankfurter does between individual and group libel. There is an interesting echo, however, from the Kunz case, decided the year before. There the law under which the license was refused was read as authorizing the commissioner to refuse those who would "ridicule or denounce any form of religious belief." Justice Frankfurter agreed with the majority that this was too vague a standard to guide the discretion of the administrative official in licensing the use of public parks.[66]

We turn next to Justice Jackson, whose lengthy dissent raises a major First Amendment issue but is in the end very difficult to follow. The major point is the suggestion that freedom of speech is different under the First Amendment measuring *federal* power than it is under the Fourteenth Amendment measuring state power.[67] He feels driven to this solution by the history of criminal libel. The history of the Sedition Act of 1798 makes it clear, he thinks, that there can be no federal criminal libel. The universality of state criminal-libel laws, many of which antedate the passage of the Fourteenth Amendment, make it equally clear, he argues, that that amendment cannot be read as prohibiting state criminal libel altogether. He is thus willing to meet the majority half-way and agree that state libel laws can be constitutional. But the apparent diplomacy of this solution which would keep high the barriers against federal seditious libel while permitting him to join the majority of the court in upholding this state law turns out not to have been Jackson's objective at all. There is another leg to his analysis: state laws, even under the generous provisions of the Fourteenth Amendment, must still satisfy the *Palko* test[68] of "ordered liberty." This means, he argues, that they must incorporate certain safeguards such as making truth a defense, letting the issue of libel go to the jury, and allowing the privilege of fair comment. The Illinois statute as applied here did none of these and is, therefore, invalid. The Jackson analysis is, however, still not exhausted: there is still clear and present danger to dispose of. This, he finds, is "the one addition to the safeguards voluntarily taken upon the states by themselves" which the Supreme Court has added. He would, therefore, "superimpose" the clear and present danger test on the normal state safeguards of jury, truth, and fair comment. And here once again, the trial wholly fails to satisfy the requirements.

The interactions between the Jackson dissent and the majority opinion yield more points than can readily be disposed of here. Two, however, are of special interest. Whereas it was a principal feature of Frankfurter's argument to treat libel as speech beneath any clear and present danger requirement, Jackson, a cool supporter of the test in *Dennis*,[69] would hold to clear and present danger as especially appropriate for cases of this sort. But the spectacular feature of Jackson's opinion is the thesis that the First Amendment has a different meaning vis à vis the states than it does vis à vis the federal government. It is a sharp reminder that free speech, too, like the Negro rights issue has its federalism aspects and strains.[70] The thesis, we should note, is later picked up by Justice Harlan in 1957 in the Roth case upholding the constitutionality of both state and federal laws regulating obscenity.[71] However, the Jackson development of it is oddly unpersuasive; his point is chiefly that there are many fewer areas of communication which the federal government has the power, as a matter of federalism, to regulate. This is probably true; it is difficult, for example, to see under what power it could enact a federal criminal-libel law. But this is an issue of allocation of federal and state power and can be handled without resort to the First Amendment as the instrument of restraint. What is more important

is the issue of allocation of power between the state
and the individual. Here, I find it difficult to accept
the Jackson distinction. Surely there cannot be one
idea of free speech essential to ordered liberty and
binding on the states, and another idea of free
speech, not so fundamental, but more stringent,
which inhibits the federal government alone. We
are having enough difficulty working out one good
theory of free speech without having the obligation
now to develop two theories—one for the state level
and one for the federal level. Further, the Court
having so recently in *Mapp* v. *Ohio*[72] and *Gideon* v.
Wainwright[73] reversed itself and held that there is
only one standard for search and seizure and for
right to counsel, it would be extraordinary for it,
for the sake of federalism, to subscribe to a two-
tier view of free speech.[74] In any event, there is a
curious lack of responsive debate between the Jackson dissent and the majority opinion. Jackson says
nothing about Frankfurter's key two-level theory of
speech and his reliance on *Chaplinsky;* Frankfurter
says nothing about the key two-tier federalism point
of Jackson.

Two final points about the Jackson opinion should
be noted. First, it could have served to put into
issue something more subtle than the simple position
that group libel is bad versus the simple position
that it cannot be regulated. His insistence that the
common-law safeguards are relevant suggests the
possibility of compromise solutions and brings to

the surface an obvious but rarely discussed point in speech theory, namely the relevance of truth. Are consciously false statements of fact constitutionally protected?

Secondly, although the case reminds him of the Sedition Act of 1798, and of Fox's Libel Act, he never pauses to challenge the assumption that individual libel and group libel can be equated. Indeed, his whole two-tier theory of the First and Fourteenth amendments is required because he wishes to accommodate individual criminal libel. In the end, although his opinion is genuinely interesting, it is not a successful answer to Frankfurter and is high evidence of how confused free-speech doctrine and theory had become even among able, concerned justices.

The Douglas dissent is the briefest of the four. It begins with an arresting reminder of why group libel is serious business:

> Hitler and his Nazis showed how evil a conspiracy could be which was aimed at destroying a race by exposing it to contempt, derision, and obloquy. I would be willing to concede that such conduct directed at a race or group in this country could be made an indictable offense. For such a project would be more than the exercise of free speech.[75]

There is the germ of a powerful idea here. The special vice of group libel has been its systematic repetitive quality; after the Dennis case it is conceivable that careful use of the doctrines of conspiracy could produce a law tailored to fit the precise sociological reality of modern group defamation.

Douglas then concedes casually, and without any effect at precision, that there might be times and circumstances when speech could be curbed properly, such as, to coin an example, "shouting fire in a school or theatre." Conspiracy and "fire" out of the way, he is now ready to state his major premise for speech cases:

> My view is that if in any case other public interests are to override the plain command of the First Amendment, *the peril of the speech must be clear and present,* leaving no room for argument, raising no doubts as to the necessity of curbing speech in order to prevent disaster.[76]

There follows a rather bland and general essay on the importance of free speech in our constitutional arrangement. Until his final paragraph, he does not address this case specifically. On two occasions he speaks of actions of the Court "in this and in other cases." The general essay is memorable, however, for what is perhaps the most emphatic statement ever made in the Court on the preferred position of speech as against the economic market place:

> Free speech, free press, free exercise of religion are placed separate and apart; they are above and beyond the police power; they are not subject

to regulation in the manner of factories, slums, apartment houses, production of oil and the like.[77]

The Beauharnais case can thus be read as marking the most intense polarity of positions on free speech within the Supreme Court. At the very time Douglas is announcing so firmly that speech has a preferred position in the constitutional hierarchy, the majority opinion of Frankfurter is announcing equally firmly that there are several well-known categories of speech that are *beneath* the First Amendment's protections, and is further announcing that the appropriate test in the instant case is whether this law "is a wilful and purposeless regulation"—a test less exacting than would be applied to purely economic regulation.

There are two other details of the Douglas opinion that deserve some mention. At the end, although recognizing that this is only one case, and that it may well be limited in the future, he nevertheless observes that it "represents a *philosophy* at war with the First Amendment." And as he moves into his final paragraph, he turns for the first time to the context of the case before him and says with notable prescience, in view of the recent *New York Times* case:

> Today a white man stands convicted for protesting in unseemly language against our decisions invalidating restrictive covenants. Tomorrow a

Negro will be hauled before a court for denouncing lynch law in heated terms.[78]

He then proceeds rhetorically to put a series of cases, apparently within the Illinois statute, on which it would have been helpful to hear the majority:

> Farm laborers in the West who compete with field hands drifting up from Mexico; whites who feel the pressure of orientals; a minority who finds employment going to members of a dominant religious group—all of these are caught in the mesh of today's decision.[79]

And he reminds us:

> Debate and argument even in the courtroom are not always calm and dispassionate—Intemperate speech is a distinctive characteristic of man.[80]

We turn finally to the dissent of Justice Black. It will be remembered that none of the dissents thus far has been responsive to the special structure of argument in the majority opinion. Justice Reed need not be since he is attacking on the quite separate grounds of vagueness and could in theory accept the Frankfurter analysis of other points. Justice Jackson evolves a new *federal* theory of the First Amendment which would give special latitude to the states to have criminal-libel laws. But then in an about-face he holds that clear and present danger is the appropriate test for such laws. And Justice Douglas finds clear and present danger the almost universal test for speech regulation and sees the instant case simply as an episode in a running battle in the Court over the preferred position of speech. What then does Justice Black do by way of meeting the Frankfurter argument?

It is perhaps appropriate to start at the very end of the Black opinion. The mood of the dissent is expressed in his exceptionally eloquent and effective close:

> If there be minority groups who hail this holding as their victory, they might consider the possible relevance of this ancient remark: Another such victory and I am undone.[81]

The first section of the dissent picks up a feature of the case which the other justices have pretty much ignored: namely, the fact that the Beauharnais leaflet was in the form of a petition to the mayor and city council. "That Beauharnais and his group were making a genuine effort to petition their elected representatives is not disputed." On this view we have not simply free speech in issue, but also that other clause of the First Amendment dealing with "the right of the people peaceably to assemble and to petition the Government for a redress of grievances." Presumably, this is an act in the official channels of government process and might be immune from any restraints of libel law. In any event, the Black opinion opens on the broadest possible grounds—the First Amendment has been so degraded by recent constitutional doctrine that even this historic privilege to petition for redress of grievances can be limited. There are echoes of the Douglas insistence that legislation affecting speech is not to be tested by mere reasonableness but by more stringent criteria, speech has a preferred position.

It is a disturbing sign of the inability of the members of the Court to talk to one another that no one responds to the point about the petition except Jackson who thinks its bona fides should also have been submitted to the jury. We just miss, therefore, getting light on the fascinating issue of how realistic the Court can permit itself to be. If it would make a difference whether the petition was genuine and not just a trick of form, can the Court penetrate the form and appraise the true motivation or must it, as it does with congressional committees, accept the official motivation?[82]

Justice Black then turns directly to the particular case before the Court. He explicitly and ably challenges the assimilation of group libel to individual libel:

> The Court condones this expansive state censorship by painstakingly analogizing it to the law of criminal libel. As a result of this refined analysis, the Illinois statute emerges labeled a group libel law. This label may make the Courts holding more

palatable for those who sustain it, but the sugar coating does not make the censorship less deadly. However tagged, the Illinois law is not the criminal libel which has been "defined, limited and constitutionally recognized time out of mind." For as "constitutionally recognized" that crime has provided for punishment of false malicious scurrilous charges against individuals not against huge groups. This limited scope of the law of criminal libel is of no small importance. It has confined state punishment to *the narrowest* of areas involving nothing more than purely private feuds. Every expansion of the law of criminal libel so as to punish matters of public concern means a corresponding invasion of the area dedicated to free expression by the First Amendment.[83]

Following the majority argument closely, Justice Black then turns to the special problems of the majority's use of the Chaplinsky case. He would distinguish it on the grounds that there individuals were involved and that here there is a genuine effort of petition. He thoughtfully observes:

> Freedom of petition, assembly, speech, and press could be greatly abridged by a practice of meticulously scrutinizing every editorial, speech, sermon or other printed matter to extract two or three naughty words on which to hang charges of group libel. The *Chaplinsky* case makes no such broad inroads on First Amendment freedoms.[84]

The final paragraphs of the dissent return to the high ground of the opening.

Whatever the danger, if any, in such public discussions, it is a danger the Founders deemed outweighed by the danger incident to the stifling of thought and speech. The court does not act on this view of the Founders.[85]

There is, however, in passing, another shrewd observation:

In other words, in arguing for or against the enactment of laws that may differently affect huge groups, it is now very dangerous indeed to say something critical of one of the groups.[86]

And again and again he recurs to his opening premise that Beauharnais was making a genuine petition for redress of grievances.

The analogies between the Douglas and Black dissents are many, as would be expected. Both utilize the particular case as an occasion to complain about the trend of recent decisions. Both argue that First Amendment issues require something different from ordinary judicial review. Both think the result in the instant case dangerous to public discussion. There is, however, one impressive difference. Douglas keys his argument to the clear and present danger test; Black never mentions it. He is well on the way to his "absolute" interpretation of First Amendment freedom. So we can now see at least four different theories of the First Amendment at work in the opinion of Frankfurter, Jackson, Douglas, and Black.

So much then for the detailed drama of the conflicting opinions. What are the more durable points to make about the case? At the outset there is a point about the strategy of the dissenters. Although Black is, to be sure, more responsive than Douglas to the facts of the case before him, they are both engaged in treating the case as one more defeat in a war of attrition against free speech and are moved therefore to argue much of their opinions on the highest and broadest, and therefore least persuasive, grounds. Given the prior decisions up to that point, they should have been able to challenge frontally the sleight-of-hand use of *Chaplinsky* so as to force some explicit consideration of a clear and present danger threshhold or at least avoid the implication that, since libel was involved, the issue of constitutionality was already foreclosed. The majority made a precise, but I think unsound, lawyer's argument for its conclusion; the dissenters chose to put in issue the entire philosophy of the First Amendment. Perhaps the pattern of challenge and response in the published opinions is a symptom of the despair of genuine communication engendered by bitter discussions in chambers. Perhaps it is true that our great dissents are written for posterity and not in any hope of meeting the majority opinion. But, I feel that it would somehow be better for the forces of freedom if the dissents were directed more to the case before the Court.

Then there is the major issue of the status and universality of the clear and present danger test for free-speech issues. The test proves an inappropriate instrument for the problem of group libel. It is too simplistic for the problem at hand. It requires the pointing to some specific evil engendered by the speech, such as a breach of peace; but although group libel may on occasion be productive of a breach of peace, this approach to it focusses on the wrong evil. Group libels would be exactly as odious, antisocial, and dangerous even though there were never to be a breach of peace. Further, if we attempt to substitute the evil of racial hatred and tension and prejudice in order to get an immediate evil, we may be talking sensibly about systematic group libel but this logical turn deprives the test of any bite; it is simply a cumbersome way of talking about the connection between legislation and its objective, talking, that is, about the reasonableness of the legislation. More important, it has never been clear that clear and present danger was offered as the criterion for *all* forms of speech problems so that we could say *any* speech which does not present a clear and present danger of overt conduct is constitutionally untouchable. The Beauharnais case is important in part, therefore, because it puts to the Court so clearly a kind of speech problem which reveals the incompleteness of a speech theory keyed exclusively to clear and present danger. And the variety of judicial responses could scarcely be greater. Frankfurter argues, in effect, if the speech does not meet the test, that the test is irrelevant and that *therefore* the speech can be regulated. Douglas argues that since the speech does not meet the test, it cannot be regulated. Reed apparently would agree with Frankfurter that group libel could be regulated, the test apart, but finds the particular Illinois statute fatally vague. Jackson would apparently agree with Frankfurter that the test is not universal but would agree with Douglas that the test is relevant at least for this kind of speech and in addition would add the complication that the proper criterion, whatever it is, should not be the same at state and federal level. Finally, Black would find that this speech cannot be regulated, but would do so without special reliance on, or even reference to, the test.

I would agree, therefore, that Frankfurter's instinct is correct in rejecting clear and present danger as the criterion here. Having granted this much, I would hasten to add that there remain, however, two serious sources of dissatisfaction with his handling of the problem. The first turns on his use of the Chaplinsky case; the second turns on his insensitivity to the analogies to seditious libel.

The reliance on *Chaplinsky* introduces what I have called elsewhere the two-level theory of the First Amendment.[87] The full significance of the innovation does not, perhaps, become apparent until

1957, when in *Roth* the Court disposes of the constitutionality of obscenity regulation by relying on
Beauharnais. It seems to me that as a matter of
constitutional speech theory, the distinction Frankfurter is here drawing is as important and far
reaching as the original announcement of clear and
present danger. Insofar as I can follow the analysis
here, it is this: There are two categories of speech—
that entitled to First Amendment scrutiny, although
after such scrutiny it may prove subject to regulation; and that so without importance or ideas that
it is virtually per se subject to regulation and raises
no constitutional issues. Fighting words we are
told in *Chaplinsky,* libel we are told in *Beauharnais,*
and obscenity we are told in *Roth* belong in this
lower echelon and that is why they can be regulated
consistently with the First Amendment.

There are several points to be made about this
doctrinal development. First, it is not clear what
the rationale behind it is. Is it that such speech is
worthless, or is it that these are historical exceptions
necessarily engrafted onto the First Amendment,
or is it simply that this is speech for which clear
and present danger is an inappropriate test? Each
of these explanations invites difficulty. Libel and
obscenity are often found in complex utterances;
the offensive words rarely stand alone; hence, it is
simply not true that all that these labels may cover
can categorically be said to be worthless. Further,

the additional protection given revolutionary speech, as over these categories, is instructive here: what is so differentially valuable about it? Nor can a satisfactory answer be found in history; the premise that any speech regulatable at the time of the adoption of the Amendment is not within that "freedom of speech," the abridging of which it prohibits, is surely difficult to maintain; and if this is not the premise, it is hard to see on what basis, as a matter of history, some categories of previously regulated speech pass muster and some do not. Further, the history has never been argued seriously in the Court;[88] and finally, with special reference to libel, there is the acute embarrassment that Fox's Libel Act was adopted the year after the First Amendment, so that on this view even its modest reforms would not be constitutionally underwritten in the United States. The two-level approach makes most sense, for reasons already suggested, if it is read as an effort to locate those categories of speech which are not to be tested under clear and present danger. But if this is Justice Frankfurter's point, it is surely a *non sequitur* to conclude that because it is speech not appropriate for the test it is therefore automatically vulnerable to regulation. The better conclusion surely would be that some other test then is called for.

Finally we may go back for a moment to the original passage in *Chaplinsky,* which is the acknowledged source of the two-level concept. This is the relevant passage in full:

> There are certain well defined and narrowly limited classes of speech, the prevention and punishment of which have never been thought to raise any Constitutional problem. These include the lewd and obscene, the profane, the libellous, and the insulting or "fighting" words—those which by their very utterance inflict injury or tend to incite to an immediate breach of the peace. It has been well observed that such utterances are no essential part of any exposition of ideas and are of such slight social value as a step to truth that any benefit that may be derived from them is clearly outweighed by the social interest in order and morality.[89]

I submit that the Court in *Beauharnais* and *Roth* has misread the above passage from *Chaplinsky,* although the language is, to be sure, not free from difficulty. To score an easy point first: the passage was written by Justice Murphy, surely a most unlikely father for a pervasive principle for limiting speech. Secondly, the facts of the Chaplinsky case make clear what the Court was thinking of. The defendant had called the sheriff "a damn Fascist etc." At the level of vulgar, abusive speech these categories run together; to call a man a "bastard," or something slightly more taboo, to his face can be classified equally well as the use of obscenity, profanity, libel, and fighting words. These are simply vulgar epithets, and it is probable that the

Court in its omnibus language about obscenity and libel meant simply to sweep them together.

That this was so is confirmed by tracing the Murphy passage back to its source. As the footnotes in *Chaplinsky* acknowledge, the passage is a paraphrase of a passage in Chafee's *Free Speech in the United States.* To score a doubly easy point, I would now observe that it is amusing to have Professor Chafee, the most devoted and concerned student of free speech in our history, and Justice Murphy, an almost extravagantly liberal judge, be the co-authors of a new line of analysis limiting speech.

This is the passage from Chafee:

> The normal criminal law is interested in preventing crimes and certain non criminal interferences with governmental functions like refusals to enlist or to subscribe to bonds. It is directed primarily against actual injuries. Such injuries are usually committed by acts, but the law also punishes a few classes of words like obscenity, profanity and gross libels upon individuals because the very utterance of such words is considered to inflict a present injury upon listeners, readers or those defamed or else to render highly probable an immediate breach of the peace. This is a very different matter from punishing words because they express ideas which are thought to cause a future danger to the State.[90]

What Chafee, and hence Murphy, is saying is really that a certain class of face to face epithets are regulatable per se because they are, so to speak, per se freighted with a clear and present danger. Hence in this very limited sense there may be a lower echelon of communication, but it is at the level of isolated epithet and nothing more; and, in any event, the rationale for it is clear and present danger. The extension, therefore, of the two-level theory to the complex utterances that might be brought within obscenity or group libel is a totally unwarranted step of doctrine, whatever we may think of the vulnerability of obscenity and libel to regulation.

I come next to my second dissatisfaction with the Frankfurter opinion, which will, I hope, bring our discussion full circle. As I see it, the Beauharnais case was a great chance for the Court to look to the status of seditious libel in American law. For me the most revealing aspect of the opinions, and particularly that of Justice Frankfurter, is the absence of any sense of the proximity of the case before them to seditious libel. The case presents almost a perfect instance of that competition among analogies which Edward Levi has emphasized as the essential circumstance of legal reasoning.[91] In the middle we have group libel and Justice Frankfurter's urging its many resemblances to individual libel. But in the other corner, almost unnoticed, we have seditious libel and only Justice Black in dissent faintly urging group libel's many resemblances to

it. If the Court's speech theory had been more
grounded, as it seems to me it should be, on the
relevance of the concept of seditious libel and less
on the analogy to the law of attempts found in the
slogan "clear and present danger," it is difficult
to believe that either the debate or the result in
Beauharnais v. *Illinois* would have been the same.
In the end, Justice Frankfurter was correct in
rejecting clear and present danger as the test for
this type of speech evil; liberated from clear and
present danger, he was, however, remarkably wrong,
as I see it, in ignoring the historic significance of
seditious libel while finding so close a connection
between individual libel and group libel.

The Beauharnais case has, I think, lived up to its
advance billing as a central document for American
free-speech theory. We must still note two very
recent developments which will serve to bring our
detailed study of the case to a close.

We turn first to the celebrated interview on the
First Amendment that Professor Edmond Cahn had
a year or so ago with Justice Black, which was
subsequently published as a "public interview" in
the *New York University Law Review.*[92] Apparently after experiences like the Beauharnais case,
Justice Black had been brooding further over the
law of libel. As a result of the interview, he was
widely reported in the public press to have announced that he had now concluded that the tort

law of defamation was unconstitutional. The interview is not a great success, and I find it difficult to
say just how far Justice Black was carrying his
opposition. He was asked by Mr. Cahn about the
law of libel and slander. His answer is primarily
about *federal* law. He did, however, say in words
which gave me hope that the concept of seditious
libel was coming back into free-speech idiom:

> As far as public libel is concerned or seditious
> libel, I have been very much disturbed sometimes
> to see that there is present an idea that because
> we have had the practice of suing individuals for
> libel, seditious libel still remains for use of govern-
> ment in this country. Seditious libel as it has been
> put into practice throughout the centuries is
> nothing in the world except the prosecution of
> people who are on the wrong side politically; they
> have said something and their group has lost and
> they are prosecuted.[93]

These issues with which we have been wrestling—
the relation of the law of libel to free speech and
more particularly the role of the concept of seditious libel—were given extraordinary currency by
an explosive decision of the Court on March 9,
1964, in the case of *New York Times* v. *Sullivan*.[94]
Perhaps it is only coincidence, but the case preserves
our central theme of First Amendment issues generated from the Negro movement. As we noted,
Justice Douglas had predicted in *Beauharnais* that
"in the next case a Negro would be haled before

the court for protesting in heated terms, lynch law
in the South." In fact, four Negro ministers, including the well-known leader Rev. Fred Shuttlesworth,
are sued along with the *New York Times* for libel
of a Montgomery, Alabama, police official as a
result of statements made in an advertisement which
the *Times* carried. If in *Beauharnais* the problem
was the application of libel laws to critics of the
Negro, in the *Times* case it is the application of the
libel laws to the Negro critics of Southern treatment
of the protest movement.

On its facts, the *Times* case seems to have been
put together by the Devil himself in order to embar-
rass the legal system. On the surface a public official is held by a state court and jury to have been
defamed by an editorial advertisement in the *Times*.
The state rule as to fair comment on public officials
requires that all supporting statements of fact be
true. In several particulars in the case the defense
of truth fails. Further, the statement does not
mention the plaintiff by name but the jury finds that
it was sufficiently of and concerning him. The jury
is instructed on both general damages and punitive
damages, and, without any showing of special dam-
age, brings in a verdict of $500,000. On the surface,
then, we have a civil libel action in which Alabama
has simply applied the majority American rule as
to comment on public officials[95] and has applied the
three great rules of Anglo-American tort of defa-

mation: (1) there is strict liability; (2) substantial general damages may be presumed from the publication of the statement without proof of more; (3) falsity may also be presumed from publication with the burden thrown on defendant to prove the full truth if he can. Some other features are perhaps less typical. The court has withdrawn from the jury the issue of whether the statement was defamatory; the connection of the statement with the plaintiff is slight; the statement was substantially true; and the damages are extremely high.

If then we consider the rules of law Alabama applied in the case, they are odd; but the oddity is one deeply engrained in centuries of Anglo-American tort law. To make the decision look more familiar, one need only compare it to the well-known English libel case in the 1930's, *Youssoupoff* v. *MGM*,[96] in which the distinguished Justice Scrutton upheld a judgment of £25,000 for a movie which suggested that a Russian princess had been raped by the mad monk Rasputin, a man, as the Court put it, "of the worst possible character."

But, this, of course, is not the whole story. The *Times* case has to be read against the sociological reality which produced it. First the publication in Alabama was tenuous in the extreme; the advertisement was addressed to the normal audience of the *Times;* it appears that less than four hundred copies of the 650,000 circulation of the *Times* were circu-

lated in Alabama and only thirty-five copies in the
county in question. Second, other suits from the
same advertisement were pending, threatening several million dollars more in damages. Third, there
is, at least in Northern eyes, something disingenuous
about the response of the Southern jury to the defamation involved; it involves the South in a showing
of moral shock at vigorous conduct countering the
Negro protest movement. In brief, although there
was perhaps a technical libel involved, the impression is that the technicality was pounced on and
exploited in Southern irritation over Northern interference in the civil-rights controversy.

Further, somehow when the interaction of the
various rules is added up in the case, the whole
seems a good deal worse than the sum of its parts.
The statement barely, if at all, can be read as re-
ferring to plaintiff; the misstatements of fact are
miniscule; the likelihood that there was any loss of
reputation to plaintiff is remote; and the damages
are extravagant. The result, if said quickly, is that
for a statement which was not published in Alabama,
which did not refer to plaintiff, and which was substantially true, the *New York Times* is being held
to pay the Alabama plaintiff half a million dollars.[97]
I have no doubt that the Court, therefore, had to
do something about the case, but I have rarely seen
a case in which an inescapably right conclusion was
so awkward to support on doctrinal grounds.

It will, to be sure, take a few years to fully digest the impact of the Court's response on existing tort and constitutional law. In brief, in a unanimous decision with, however, separate concurring opinions by Justice Black and Justice Goldberg, the Court upset the judgments and held: (1) that the Alabama rule as to fair comment on public officials in civil-libel suits was unconstitutional under the First and Fourteenth amendments; (2) that an appropriate rule would require showing actual malice to defeat the privilege; (3) that as a matter of constitutional fact, there was in the existing record insufficient evidence of such malice; (4) that again as a matter of constitutional fact there was insufficient evidence that the statement was of and concerning the plaintiff since it is now a matter of constitutional importance that impersonal statements about government policy may not be transmuted into individual libel and hence subjected to legal sanctions. Both Justice Black and Justice Goldberg argued that the Court had not gone far enough and that an *absolute* privilege of comment on public officials was required.[98]

From the point of view of an old teacher of the law of defamation, the case is especially fascinating and goes a long way toward giving us special status by turning defamation into a branch of constitutional law. What is arresting is that the Court now suddenly decides that the long-standing majority rule as to fair comment on public officials is unconstitutional[99] and that the state of mind of the defendant is now a constitutional fact which the Court presumably will review *de novo*. Further examination of these aspects of the case, however, will have to wait another day. Our business is with its relationship to *Beauharnais* and to free-speech doctrine.

What criterion, we may ask, tells the Court that the Alabama libel law is unconstitutional under the First Amendment? In many ways, the most unusual thing about the majority opinion of Justice Brennan is that it reads as though we are starting all over again to build a free-speech doctrine afresh. There is not a word of clear and present danger or of balancing. The key source of insight for the Court, following closely the very able brief for the defendants on which Professor Wechsler participated, comes from seditious libel—or rather from what one might better call the negative radiations from seditious libel. Neither factual error nor defamatory content serve, we are told, "to remove the constitutional shield from criticism of official conduct." Then follows a profound and welcome sentence, lifted literally from the Wechsler brief: "This is the lesson to be drawn from the great controversy over the Sedition Act of 1798, *which first crystallized a national awareness of the central meaning of the First Amendment*."[100] We are given

a several-page discussion of the history of the Act
and the closest thing yet to an official adjudication
of its unconstitutionality: "Although the Sedition
Act was never tested in this Court, the attack upon
its validity has carried the day in the court of
history."[101]

The notable precision of this language does not
quite conceal the jump that is being made over the
troublesome history of the Sedition Act proper. The
Court, following Professor Wechsler, is careful not
to say that the Sedition Act was unconstitutional
when enacted and that history so shows. Rather,
the proposition is the sophisticated one that the
Sedition Act is unconstitutional now, whatever the
history of its adoption, and that this is shown by
the history of its reception. Since its adoption, it
has been tried in the "court of history" and found
wanting.[102] This is pretty heady argument, and we
will need time to digest it fully. If the avoidance
of seditious libel is the "central meaning" of the
First Amendment, the rest of the Court's argument
flows easily: the Alabama rule literally applied legal
sanctions to criticism of official conduct. Its sanctions, although merely civil and not criminal, were,
in fact, more stringent and inhibiting than the
penalties of the Sedition Act. Therefore, the Alabama rule, like the Sedition Act of 1798, is bad.
In fact, the puzzle in this logic is why the Court
did not go all the way with Black and Goldberg

and grant an absolute privilege rather than stopping
with a privilege defeasible on the showing of actual
malice.[103]

One is tempted to observe that the very curious
facts of the *Times* case forced the Court back to
the discovery of a basic truth about the First
Amendment, namely that the core of its constitutional protection must be to guard against treating
seditious libel as an offense and that we are now to
work out toward a more complete theory from there.

While the opinion is devoted primarily to the
problem before it—that of criticism of a public
official—there are strong suggestions in it of an
extremely broad and generous view which is highly
reminiscent of the position of Alexander Meiklejohn.
The Court is impressed, again following a point
urged in the briefs, by the analogy of the absolute
privilege in the law of libel of high government
officials, a privilege they had recently reaffirmed with
force in *Barr* v. *Matteo*.[104] The rationale for the
extreme protection of the high ranking official has
been that the very threat of litigation might inhibit his performance of important public duties.
"Analogous considerations," the Court now tells,
"support the privilege for the citizen-critic of government. It is as much his duty to criticize as it is
the official's duty to administer. . . . It would give
public servants an unjustified preference over the
public they serve, if critics of official conduct did

not have a fair equivalent of the immunity granted
to the officials themselves."[105] This, as Mr. Meiklejohn pointed out to us all some fifteen years ago,
is a fine analogy for free-speech doctrine;[106] taken
seriously, however, it would move the Court well
past the boundaries of the present case. It would
yield the full Meiklejohn position that there is an
absolute privilege for the citizen when engaged in
his official business of discussing public issues of
any sort.

There is a second major theoretical component of
the majority opinion. For the first time the Court
takes an explicit position on the relevance of truth
and falsity. While it perhaps intends its comments
to be limited to the problem before it, the Court
goes a long way toward making truth and falsity
irrelevant. This, of course, had always been the
operating rule with respect to statements of doctrine.
Free speech was always somewhat broader than the
freedom to circulate the truth. As Justice Stewart
put it so effectively in *Kingsley Pictures* a few
years back:

> This argument misconceives what it is that the
> Constitution protects. Its guarantee is not confined
> to the expression of ideas that are conventional or
> shared by a majority. It protects advocacy of the
> opinion that adultery may sometimes be proper,
> no less than advocacy of socialism or the single
> tax. And in the realm of ideas it protects expres-
> sion which is eloquent no less than that which is
> unconvincing.[107]

Statements of fact might, however, be thought to be on a different footing. But the Court takes a dim view of rules limiting the privilege to truthful statements of fact. It is moved by two considerations. First, the likelihood that in vigorous public debate errors will be made. The Court quotes with approval the dictum from *Cantwell* v. *Connecticut* on religious controversy, that "to persuade others to his point of view the pleader, as we know, at times, resorts to exaggeration, to vilification of men who have been, or are, prominent in church or state and even to false statement."[108] And then the Court adds that "erroneous statement is inevitable in free debate and must be protected if the freedoms of expression are to have the breathing space they need to survive." Secondly, the Court is moved by the difficulties of proving truth in these matters and, therefore, of putting the speaker to the risk of proof before fallible judges, juries, or administrative officials. It suggests, therefore, the interesting point that one rationale behind freedom of speech is the distrust of the law's own capacity to make needed discriminations; we must in effect over-protect speech in order to protect it at all.

It is striking that while the *Times* case reverses the trend of the Beauharnais case, it does not in any sense revive clear and present danger as a key speech formula. Indeed, as we have already noted, the Court finds it virtually unnecessary to mention it. Perhaps more than any other circumstance this is indicative of the curious present state of doctrine. A prime argument for the defense in the *Times* case was the analogy of the contempt by publication cases. The argument was that contempt was really simply defamation of judges. Since the Court had so emphatically in the celebrated Bridges,[109] Pennekamp,[110] and Craig [111] cases limited the power to punish for contempt, it was argued that other public officials should not be more shielded from criticism than are judges. The analogy is apt. What is odd, however, is that the three contempt cases are analyzed entirely in terms of clear and present danger; it is the use of the test and not any analogy to seditious libel that has carried the day when contempt was involved. And as recently as 1962 in *Wood* v. *Georgia,*[112] another contempt case, the Court repeated its adherence to clear and present danger as the proper criterion for limiting defamation of judges. In the *Times* case the Court follows the defense and cites the contempt cases as a key analogy, but nevertheless does not talk of clear and present danger.

What has happened to the *Beauharnais* precedent in all this? It is, after all, only twelve years old. The two cases can be reconciled, although the one seems to tell us that libel is beneath any First Amendment concerns while the other seems to tell us libel is at the heart of First Amendment concerns.[113] If we define seditious libel technically and restrict it to public officials, the cases can, of course, be reconciled. In *Beauharnais,* Negroes and not public officials were the subject of criticism; in the *Times* case the subject is a public official. And as the Court now gratefully notes, Justice Frankfurter had been careful and foresighted enough in a footnote in *Beauharnais* to indicate that "very different" issues would arise were public officials involved in that case.[114] So restated, the principle is that libel, like fighting words, is beneath the First Amendment protections except for libel of officials, avoidance of sanctions for which is at the center of the Amendment's concerns.

Further, it is probable that the case spells the doom for any future growth of the Jackson-Harlan view that free speech has a different meaning at the state and federal levels. Indeed, a chief embarrassment of the *Times* case is that the Court is upsetting so much familiar state libel law, much of which must have been in force when the Fourteenth Amendment was adopted; it, therefore, was an especially propitious time for use of the two-tier theory. Yet its current champion, Justice Harlan, concurs without a murmur, although the Jackson effort with respect to libel in *Beauharnais* which Harlan liked so much in *Roth,* would surely have been more persuasive here.

The *Times* case brings our story to a happy close. The chance that was dismally flubbed in

Beauharnais is now gallantly realized. At the very least, the *Times* case will have the benign effect of fencing-off *Beauharnais* as a precedent, and hopefully of dampening forever enthusiasm for the two-level theory. Far more important, it may well have the effect of stimulating the building of a new speech theory by analogies radiating outward from the evils of making seditious libel a crime—a theory working outward from "the central meaning of the First Amendment." And in any event, Justice Brennan, in the course of his opinion, has enriched us with a splendid sentence, possibly the most felicitous expression on free speech yet. We have, he tells us, "a profound national commitment to the principle that debate on public issues should be uninhibited, robust, and wide-open."[115]

II

Anonymity, Privacy,
and Freedom of Association

IN THIS LECTURE we move to a different sector of
First Amendment theory. Our problems arise
out of what has been called the "counterattack of
the South." In brief, we are to look closely at the
response of the Supreme Court in a series of cases
involving specific efforts by Southern states to limit,
control, and discipline the NAACP. Unlike the libel
issues in which the connection was perhaps tangen-
tial, here we have issues that are central to the whole
Negro movement.

We are touching, too, a live nerve of the law and
a point of exciting growth. Certainly, the cases are
coming to the Court at a dizzy space. Of the six
Supreme Court cases that will chiefly concern us,
the oldest dates from 1957, the rest are after 1960,
and the two most important are from 1963.[116]

As we try to fit the results of these cases into the
existing legal framework, we have an acute sense
of history repeating itself albeit with a new twist.
The great civil liberties issues of the postwar decade

centered on the national efforts to curb the domestic communist conspiracy. It is not entirely poetry to say that the NAACP is from the standpoint of the beleaguered South a second domestic conspiracy aiming at a revolution. And the Southern states have responded to the challenge by seeking to adapt the legal methods used to fight communism. Thus far the tactic has been highly unsuccessful. There is, therefore, little suspense in the story we are about to tell; the outcome is wholly predictable. The Court will protect the NAACP.

But for students of legal institutions there is more to this story than the bare outline of the plot. We have three special and interrelated interests: first, exploring the limits of judicial realism to determine to what extent the Court may second guess the motivation of the South; secondly, testing to what extent the Court can avoid the appearance of a simple blunt voting for the Negro cause; and finally, to bring us back to our main theme since the cases go off on First Amendment grounds, analyzing what these fresh problems and decisions add to free-speech theory.

One of the most distinctive features of the Negro revolution has been its almost military assault on the Constitution via the strategy of systematic litigation. In brief, by forcing its controversies into court, it has accelerated mightily the evolving of legal doctrine defining Negro rights. Thus the first

great step in the movement has been the effort to
make the United States Supreme Court confront
the Negro's constitutional claims and grievances and
give the Negro his constitutional due. There has
been much speculation in the philosophy of law about
the sources of legal growth; here, however, the
stimulus is clear. Here there has been no waiting
for the random and mysterious process by which
controversies are finally brought to the Court; there
has been rather a marshaling of cases, a timing of
litigation, a forced feeding of legal growth. This
has been a brilliant use of democratic *legal* process,
and its success has been deservedly spectacular. I
am old-fashioned enough to read the development,
not as political pressure on the Court which then
as a political institution responded, but rather as a
strategy to trap democracy in its own decencies. The
Negro rights in an important sense were always
there. What was needed was a strategy for bringing them to light. The agency responsible for this
remarkable development and use of law has been
the NAACP.

The NAACP was estblished in 1909 and incorpo-
rated in New York in 1911 as a not-for-profit
membership corporation.[117] The original charter
statement of its purposes is still notably timely:

> That the principal objects for which the corpora-
> tion is formed are voluntarily to promote equality
> of rights and eradicate caste or race prejudice

among the citizens of the United States; to advance the interests of colored citizens; to secure for them impartial suffrage; and to increase their opportunities for securing justice in the courts, education for their children, employment according to their ability and complete equality before the law.

To ascertain and publish all facts bearing upon these subjects and to take any lawful action thereon; together with any and all things which may be lawfully done by a membership corporation organized under the laws of New York for the further advancement of these objects.

It has branches in some forty-six states and well over 1,000 unincorporated branches in all. It has approximately 250,000 members or about 2 per cent of the national Negro population. It is financed by annual dues which are set at a minimum of $2.00 per year. In recent years its annual income has been around $500,000. Half of the income is retained for use at the national office in New York and half is retained by the local branch. Since 1940, there has been in addition the NAACP Legal Defense and Educational Fund, which is financed solely by contributions solicited from the community at large; in recent years, the total income of the fund has averaged around $250,000. The NAACP is thus an organization not easy to place among American organizations: it is not a trade association, or a union; it has important differences from the American Civil Liberties Union; while it engages in educational and lobbying activities, its principal thrust in recent years has been the supporting of civil-rights litigation. It has legal staffs at the various state levels available for civil-rights cases. If the NAACP takes a case, it finances the total expenses, directly paying the lawyers a modest per diem. There is some controversy as to just how aggressive the NAACP has been in recruiting cases and in controlling them once begun.[118] But in any event it has commanded a large staff of able lawyers specially experienced in civil-rights litigation, and its propaganda and financial support have been an indispensable stimulus to the litigation that has occurred. One last detail may also prove relevant for later discussion: since 1957, there is evidence that both membership and contributions have declined somewhat, especially in the South.

It is said that the organization expended some $200,000 in the litigation which culminated in *Brown* v. *Board of Education* in 1954. And in the decade since, it has been particularly active in school-integration litigation in the South.[119] In a nutshell, to a South hostile to the segregation decision, the NAACP has appeared, and accurately, as a militant army led by lawyers determined to see to it that "all deliberate speed" will have some meaning.

The Southern efforts to tame the NAACP, as far as one can tell from reading cases, have taken two basic forms. First, there have been some efforts to directly control it; but more frequently the tactic has been indirect, centering chiefly on compelling disclosure of membership lists. In both forms these efforts have engendered controversies which have reached the Supreme Court and the resolution of which has significantly involved First Amendment considerations. We will turn first to the direct control issues.

We begin then with *Shelton* v. *McKinley*,[120] a decision in June, 1959, of the federal district court for the Eastern District of Arkansas. One component of the case is a year later to wend its way to the Supreme Court as *Shelton* v. *Tucker*,[121] but it is the other feature, the one which the district court disposes of, that is relevant at the moment. In 1959, the Arkansas legislature enacted a statute making it unlawful for any member of the NAACP to be employed by the state or any of its subdivisions or agencies; a non-NAACP affidavit was required as a condition for public employment.

The purpose of the legislation was announced in the preamble to the statute, which the district court summarized as follows:

> The operative sections of this statute are preceded by a preamble the gist of which is that the NAACP has been guilty of creating racial strife and turmoil in the State of Arkansas; that it has threatened progress in race relations in the State; that it has striven to stir up dissatisfaction and unrest among Negroes, and that because of its

purposes and activities membership therein is incompatible with "the peace tranquility and progress all citizens have a right to enjoy."[122]

And lest anyone should miss the communist analogy, the court further tells us:

The preamble also contains a recitation that the Special Education Committee of the Arkansas Legislative Council has found that the NAACP "is captive of the international communist conspiracy."

In a familiar series of cases on anti-communist measures, the Court had previously held that a member of the Communist Party could be made ineligible for public employment and for teaching.[123] One would have expected that a court dealing with the NAACP analogue would turn to the problem of distinguishing these cases, to the implications for free association and free speech of sanctions such as this, and, finally, to the implications for the Court's obligation to protect the *Brown* decision. The Arkansas district court does hold the statute unconstitutional and thus offers a gratifying instance of the neutrality and independence of federal judges even though they are members of troubled Southern communities. The logic by which it does so, however, seems at first blush ironic. The court relies on *Weiman* v. *Updegraff*[124] in which, it will be recalled, the Supreme Court had invalidated an oath for state teachers. The oath had required non-

membership in the Communist Party and had thus
served to render inelegible all members of the Party
without regard to whether they had knowledge of
its purposes or not. It was this absence of *scienter*
which the Supreme Court held was the fatal flaw
in the statute and which made it unconstitutional in
imposing arbitrary conditions on public employment
in the sensitive area of teaching. The Arkansas
court does not use *Weiman,* as it might have, to
argue that non-membership in NAACP is an equally
arbitrary condition for public employment. Rather it
uses the case for the *scienter* point. "The statute,"
the court tells us, "is clearly unconstitutional since
it makes mere membership in NAACP a ground for
dismissal from, or a declaration of ineligibility
for public employment, regardless of whether the
employee or applicant had any knowledge of or
sympathy with the aims and purposes of the organization as declared by the Legislature, or had actively
participated in the activities found by the Legislature to be antisocial and undesirable or whether
he was completely innocent of such knowledge,
sympathy, or participation and had joined and
was desirous of maintaining his membership in
the Association out of sympathy with its publicly
announced objectives which are clearly lawful."[125]

The court's statement needs to be read twice. At
first reading the court seems to have said that
the law is bad because Negro members of the

NAACP are indiscriminately barred from employment
whether or not they know its purposes; so read it
is a stunning example of the legal mind at work in
a vacuum. On second reading, however, it is apparent that the court has been most skillful and diplo-
matic. It is confronted with a preamble containing
legislative findings that the NAACP is engaged in
seriously antisocial activities. It is awkward for
the court to take judicial notice that those findings
are dubious; if the findings are accepted, the statute
barring members in such an antisocial group from
public employment would seem constitutional on the
basis of the prior communist cases. The court
neatly side-steps this dilemma by holding that the
employment bar must be restricted to those who
know these antisocial purposes of the NAACP. The
Arkansas legislature has in the end outsmarted
itself. In reaching for evil purposes in the NAACP
which would justify barring its members from employment, it has run afoul of the awkward fact that
it will be impossible to find any members with sufficient knowledge of *those* purposes to satisfy the
Weiman requirement.[126]

The case thus introduces a theme that will persist
throughout our discussion: The intense difference
between national and regional perspectives on the
race issue. Does the NAACP create racial strife in
Arkansas? Does it stir up dissatisfaction among
Negroes? Does it threaten progress in race relations

in the state? Is there any way of giving a *neutral* answer to such questions? And can the law deal with the controversies in this area without assuming an answer one way or the other?

The attack takes a slightly different turn in *Louisiana* v. *NAACP*,[127] which was decided by the United States Supreme Court in May, 1961. Again, only one aspect of the case concerns us at present. A recent Louisiana statute required that "non-trading associations" affiliated with out-of-state groups must, as a condition to doing business in the state, file an annual affidavit that none of the officers of the affiliate is a member of any "Communist, Communist-front or subversive organization as cited by the House Un-American Activities Committee or the United States Attorney." In a brief unanimous decision the Court invalidated the statute. Presumably the strategy here was to utilize the penalties for filing false affidavits; in any event, the NAACP branch in Louisiana declined to file and this litigation ensued.

It will be remembered that the Court had held in *Douds*[128] that non-communist affidavits could be required of officers of unions seeking the privileges of the National Labor Relations Act; it might not seem extravagant for a state to impose a comparable burden on foreign associations.

There are, to be sure, some difficulties on the surface of the law. The non-membership clause is highly ambiguous; and it is not clear what the special threat of communism is to non-trading associations—one suspects that the NAACP will turn out to be the only such organization with out-of-state affiliation in Louisiana. The Supreme Court, however, elects to dispose of the law summarily and on quite different grounds.

In an opinion by Justice Douglas, the Court notes that the national NAACP has some forty-eight directors, twenty vice presidents, and ten executive officers, few of whom reside in Louisiana. "It is not consonant with due process to require a person to swear to a fact that he cannot be expected to know or alternatively to refrain from a wholly lawful activity." There is nothing wrong with the principle invoked by the Court; it has the ring of an axiom. The question is whether it would be that difficult for the branch organization to comply. Perhaps the Court has simply capitalized on the ineptness of the Louisiana draftsmen who did not require that the officers of the affiliate file affidavits themselves but that the branch office file on their behalf. The case, however, suggests a disturbing possibility which we shall later encounter in the Gibson case[129] of pursuing the NAACP under the guise of pursuing Communists.

We come then to the major case dealing with the direct attack, *NAACP* v. *Button*,[130] decided in January, 1963. The case involves the response of Virginia; and this time the line of attack is both more sophisticated and relevant; it is aimed at the activities of the NAACP in recruiting litigants and litigation; the objective is not to ban the NAACP but to slow down its litigating. The disposition at the level of the Supreme Court is of high interest and makes a notable First Amendment point, and this time the justices are not unanimous.

The history of the litigation, before it gets to the Court, is complex, but can be sketched sufficiently for present purposes. Initially there were five Virginia statutes, all passed in 1956 at a special session of the legislature called by the governor explicitly for the purpose of dealing with the crisis created by the school segregation decision. Two of the statutes, Chapters 31 and 32, dealt with registration analogous to the Lobbying Act, while the other three, Chapters 33, 35, and 36, dealt with unlawful practice of law aspects. Litigation was begun in the federal district court for the Eastern District of Virginia before a three-judge court by a suit by NAACP against various state officials seeking a declaratory judgment as to the constitutionality of the five statutes. In *NAACP* v. *Patty*,[131] in an elaborate opinion, the district court held Chapters 31, 32, and 35 unconstitutional but abstained from passing on Chapters 33 and 36 until the Virginia courts had had a chance to construe them.

The ruling of the three-judge court was appealed directly to the Supreme Court; and in *Harrison* v. *NAACP*,[132] decided in June, 1959, the Court, speaking through Mr. Justice Harlan, vacated the judgment on the grounds that the etiquette of federalism required that the Virginia courts should be given a chance to construe all five of the statutes before the federal courts intervened. This was especially true, said Justice Harlan, since the statutes were ambiguous and might be construed by the state courts so as to avoid constitutional issues. At a time when the sense of national intervention in Southern affairs must be intensely felt in the South, this federal gesture is an arresting ceremony of restraint. The case is enlivened by a dissent by Justice Douglas, who argues that the case is to be placed, as the district court had done, in the context of a move of massive resistance by Virginia to the segregation decision. In this context there is no longer any basis for being so polite to Virginia; this is war! Justice Douglas says angrily: "Where state laws make such an assault as these do on our decisions and a State has spoken defiantly against the constitutional rights of the citizens, reasons for showing deference to local institutions vanish."[133]

The case then goes back to the Virginia courts. The two registration chapters and Chapter 35 are held unconstitutional by a three-judge state trial court; Chapter 36 is held unconstitutional by the Virginia Supreme Court in *NAACP* v. *Harrison*[134] in September, 1960. We thus have another example of the independence of the judiciary; here is a sizable fraction of the Virginia massive resistance plan being invalidated by the courts of Virginia.[135] Chapter 33 of the original five statutes thus alone survives, and it is this unit which goes to the United States Supreme Court in the Button case.

The Supreme Court strikes down Chapter 33, so that in the end no part of the five-pronged Virginia challenge to the NAACP has survived constitutional challenge in the courts. The majority opinion in the Supreme Court is by Justice Brennan; there is a concurring opinion by Justice Douglas; there is a brief partial dissent by Justice White; and a careful and impressive dissent by Justice Harlan.

It is not easy to pin down precisely what is the range of disagreement in the Court because the soliciting activities of the NAACP include so wide a variety of moves. The majority does not deny that the state may, on behalf of legal ethics, at some point regulate the stimulating of litigation; the dissent does not deny that there are important limits on how far the state may go. In the end three facts seem critical: (1) the soliciting by the NAACP of litigation for its own lawyers; (2) the financing of cases by the NAACP which its own lawyers handle; (3) the control of litigation by the NAACP once it has begun. The Virginia Supreme Court had ruled that under the statute the petitioner was free to advocate vigorously that Negroes assert their legal rights by litigating and that the petitioner was free to assist financially people who choose to litigate. What was prohibited was the soliciting of cases for NAACP lawyers, the financing of cases for NAACP lawyers, and the intervention of the NAACP between lawyer and client in the control of the litigation. Presumably much of the effectiveness of the NAACP resides in this area of dispute. Unless the NAACP goes out and signs up the client, pays for the case, and delivers the client to one of its expert lawyers, it will be unable to recruit the needed flow of litigation. Unless it can, as general policy, control the timing and line of attack in the litigation once it is begun, its grand strategy of war by lawsuit will be frustrated. And finally, unless it can do both of these, it will be unable to keep a formidable cadre of specially trained lawyers available for the purposes of civil-rights litigation.

The case thus raises a profound question for our scheme of constitutional adjudication. Who is the client in a case affecting great constitutional issues? It has been fundamental to our doctrines of judicial review to take seriously the requirement of standing and the requirement that there be an actual case or controversy that requires adjudication.[136] Yet often the great constitutional issues involve only modest private interests; in *Kunz* v. *New York*,[137] the controversy was over the payment of a ten dollar fine. There is, therefore, often a great discrepancy between the private interest of the individual litigant which produces the controversy and the large public interest in the issue he raises. To some extent, this public interest has been satisfied by the use of the amicus brief;[138] and in recent years, particularly in the civil-rights cases, the United States itself has played a major role. Thus, in the Lombard[139] case, for example, or in the Brown case, the solicitor-general has intervened as an amicus and argued. Further, the proposed Civil Rights Bill has had several sections calling for an active role by the attorney-general in litigation to implement enforcement.[140] Finally, we have for ten years or more been familiar with the use of administrative agencies like the New York SCAD in the area of civil rights; in effect, the agency is empowered to litigate on behalf of the aggrieved minority.[141] A *Yale Law Journal* note some years ago aptly called the NAACP a "private attorney general."[142] There is no secret as to what, in fact, its role is; it provides an effective stimulus to the litigating of civil-rights issues; in reality, the NAACP is the client. The problem posed in the Button case, however, is whether this role can be regulated by a state, using traditional notions of solicitation, champerty, maintenance, and barratry, whatever the actual motivation behind the regulation.

Before turning to the majority opinion of Justice Brennan, a word about the special concurring, and again angry, opinion of Justice Douglas, which picks

up this problem of the motivation. Since both the
majority and the dissent are concerned with the
state's traditional interest in legal ethics, Justice
Douglas may have added his few words simply to
put on record what the case was really about. In
any event, he repeats the gist of his opinion in the
1959 version of the same case where his point, it
will be recalled, had been that there was no need for
the federal courts to abstain out of deference. He
documents the fact that the legislation in question
arose as part of the massive resistance of Virginia
to the *Brown* decision and that six other Southern
states have passed comparable laws following the
decision in *Brown*. This time, however, his brief
opinion leaves somewhat unclear just what he is
arguing follows from this. Does this context make
unconstitutional state regulation that would otherwise be valid? Are we to infer that the statutes
will be used only against the NAACP and are bad for
that reason? Or is there lurking a premise that the
Court can protect the *Brown* decision by striking
down moves which are designed to impair it, on
analogy to contempt of court? We seem to have
here a curious instance in which the accuracy of the
realism does not help the legal analysis.

The majority opinion of Justice Brennan finding
the statute, as construed by the Virginia Supreme
Court, unconstitutional appears to break exciting
new ground. The first premise is that litigation is

for the Negro today a First Amendment activity.
It is a kind of protest, a kind of vigorous advocacy,
a kind of political expression. We quote at length:

> The First Amendment also protects vigorous
> advocacy, certainly of lawful ends, against govern-
> mental intrusion. . . . In the context of NAACP
> objectives, litigation is not a technique of resolv-
> ing private differences; it is a means for achieving
> the lawful objectives of equality of treatment by
> all government, federal, state and local for the
> members of the Negro community in this country.
> It is thus a form of political expression. Groups
> which find themselves unable to achieve their ob-
> jectives through the ballot frequently turn to the
> courts.
> We need not, in order to find constitutional
> protection for the kind of cooperative organi-
> zational activity disclosed by this record . . .
> subsume such activity under a narrow, literal
> conception of freedom of speech, petition or assem-
> bly. For there is no longer any doubt that the
> First and Fourteenth Amendments protect certain
> forms of orderly group activity. . . . The NAACP
> is not a conventional political party; but the liti-
> gation it assists while serving to vindicate the legal
> rights of members of the American Negro com-
> munity, at the same time and perhaps more im-
> portantly, makes possible the distinctive contri-
> bution of a minority group to the ideas and
> beliefs of our society. For such a group, associa-
> tion for litigation may be the most effective form
> of political association.[143]

The Court thus offers a generous view of the
range of First Amendment protection, a view which

seems to me indisputably correct although the Court
had never previously been given an appropriate
occasion for announcing it. Further, the Court is
unanimous in adding litigation to the First Amendment. Justice Harlan in dissent affirms this part
of the majority's argument:

> Freedom of expression embraces more than the
> right of the individual to speak his mind. It
> includes also his right to advocate and his right
> to join with his fellows in an effort to make that
> advocacy effective. . . . And just as it includes
> the right jointly to petition the legislature for
> redress of grievances . . . so it must include the
> right to join together for purposes of obtaining
> judicial redress.[144]

But having started out so gallantly, the opinion
turns statesmanlike. It does not hold directly that
the recruitment and control of litigation by the
NAACP, as it now does it, is constitutionally privileged activity. Rather it retreats to the vagueness
of the statute as construed by the Virginia court
and finds some fatal flaws. What is newsworthy is
the Court's move in dusting off the not recently
admired precedent in *Thornhill*[145] so that it can find
the Virginia statute bad on its face, apart from its
application to the particular activities of the NAACP.
The critical premise for the majority is found in
the following language: "We read the Virginia
Supreme Court . . . as proscribing any arrangement by which prospective litigants are advised to

seek the assistance of particular attorneys." The breadth and uncertainty of this construction creates risks for lawyers and non-lawyers alike so that "there inheres in the statute the gravest danger of smothering all discussion looking to the eventual litigation on behalf of the rights of members of an unpopular minority."[146]

Justice Harlan in sharp dissent on this point reads the Virginia court as clearly barring only solicitation of cases by the NAACP for NAACP lawyers and adds that to conclude otherwise "savors almost of disrespect to the Virginia Supreme Court of Appeals. . . . "

Simply as an exercise in reading words, Justice Harlan seems to me to have the better of the argument thus far. But the argument does not end here. Justice Brennan has another premise borrowed from the burst of realism of Justice Douglas. The argument now becomes one that, given the climate of opinion in the South in civil-rights litigation, lack of precision in the wording of a statute regulating such litigation is doubly threatening, "the statute may easily . . . become a weapon of oppression however even handed its terms appear. Its mere existence could well freeze out of existence all such activity on behalf of the civil rights of Negro citizens."[147]

In this context, Justice Harlan's talk of "savoring of disrespect" to the Virginia court has a hollow ring. This is not an old law regulating legal ethics in Virginia from time immemorial; it is a new law designed in 1956 as part of an elaborate scheme of laws to meet the crisis of the segregation decision. And somehow, as Justice Brennan insists, this fact has something to do with predictions as to how it will be construed. Nor are we persuaded by Justice Harlan's closing admonition that it will, of course, be open to petitioners to show at some later date that the law is being enforced in a discriminatory fashion.

This collision of views on the apparently colorless question of construing a statute indicates once again how pervasive and indeed corrosive the strains and tensions of the race issue are for the legal system. If the Court ignores the motivation of the South in these cases, it risks deciding great issues in a vacuum and giving us a parody of legal wisdom; yet if it acknowledges the motivation of the South, it risks giving constitutional litigation the appearance of civil war and of giving us a parody of legal neutrality. The problem is real because it is of profound importance to the Negro cause that it not merely win its cases in a court but that it win them from a just court.

One wonders, however, whether the Court had to reach this impasse in the instant case. Justice Brennan does not seem to have had the courage of his First Amendment convictions; thus his opinion

invites the inference that the state can limit the
NAACP from vigorously recruiting cases for its own
staff by offering to subsidize the litigation which it
will then basically control once it has begun. Hence,
to avoid saying this, he must rest his decision on
the ambiguity of the statute and on the realistic
likelihood of its breadth being exploited in a hostile
South. Would it not have been possible for him
to stand on his First Amendment point and to
hold that recruiting of constitutional litigation with
vigor is a protected activity, so that even on Justice
Harlan's construction the Virginia statute violates
the First Amendment? Certainly the legal ethics of
fomenting litigation has to be re-examined in light
of the needs of constitutional litigation.

In some degree this examination is begun by
Justices Brennan and Harlan in the remainder of
their opinions and debate. Even if at some level
of activity recruiting litigation is a First Amendment activity, the problem then arises of measuring
the state's interest in regulating against the interest
in freedom. We thus reach the familiar First
Amendment issue of what is to be the appropriate
test? Both judges appear to agree that balancing
rather than any form of clear and present danger
is called for, relying in good part on the disclosure
cases such as *NAACP* v. *Alabama*[148] and *Bates* v.
Little Rock,[149] which we shall turn to in detail in
the latter part of our discussion.[150]

The issue the justices put to themselves is whether in this area the state can show a "subordinating interest which is compelling"—this apparently being the new formula. One might expect the answer to be "yes" since we are in the area of control of the bar and legal ethics. Justice Brennan, however, finds the state's interest wanting when placed on the constitutional scales. He sharply distinguishes the traditional concerns of legal ethics on several grounds: (1) they involve "malicious intent"; (2) they involve pecuniary gain; (3) they involve a conflict of interests; (4) they involve unfair competition for law business. Not surprisingly he has little difficulty in establishing that the activities of the NAACP fall outside of each of these concerns. With admirable irony, he observes re the last point about competition: "Lawsuits attacking racial discrimination at least in Virginia are neither very profitable nor very popular. They are not an object of competition among Virginia lawyers." He therefore concludes "that although the petitioner has amply shown that its activities fall within the First Amendment's protections, the State has failed to advance any substantial regulatory interest in the form of substantive evils flowing from petitioner's activities which can justify the broad prohibitions which it has imposed." [151]

The total Brennan opinion thus unfortunately leaves some confusion as to its structure. There

are arguably two independent grounds on which
Justice Brennan condemns the statute once he has
brought litigation within the family of First Amendment activities. The first is that the statute as construed prohibits the innocuous act of simply advising
a person of their rights and recommending an attorney; hence, under *Thornhill,* it is bad on its face
regardless of whether the actual activities of the
NAACP would be constitutionally privileged under a
narrower statute. The second is that even the actual
activities of NAACP in recruiting and controlling litigation are—because of their high purposes, lack of
pecuniary motivation, and absence of interference
with competition—such as to fall outside the traditional concerns of the state in regulating legal ethics
and such as to leave the state on balance with no
compelling subordinating interest justifying their
impairment.

Once again Justice Harlan is in sharp dissent.
The various distinctions the majority has offered
to escape the formidable tradition of state regulation in the area of legal ethics are, we are told, "too
facile." One cannot but sympathize with Justice
Harlan in his desire to treat race law cases impar-
tially and even handedly like other controversies.
But on this occasion, at least, the effort seems to
me, with all due respect, to be a disaster. First it
shows, I submit, what is wrong with the balancing
approach as Justice Harlan would use it in First

Amendment matters. We are told that the Court's task is not to weigh the wisdom of the state's policy but simply "to determine the extent of the state's legitimate interest." But surely at some point, not too remote, the unwisdom of the state's policy undermines the legitimate interest of the state. Or to put this another way, the legitimate interest of a state in foolish legislation is difficult to isolate. And this is apart from two other difficulties this case presses on the court: (1) Is the sincerity of the state's avowed interest to be scrutinized? (2) Is the magnitude of the state's interest to be closely weighed against the magnitude of infringement of freedom involved? The instant case furnishes a strong example of the difficulty. Justice Harlan considers the possible conflict of interest between the NAACP lawyer and his client, given the control of grand strategy the NAACP wishes to retain. He then takes solemnly the state's protestation that it is this concern which has motivated its effort to regulate in 1956. And finally he weighs this against the impairment of NAACP activity that will result if the statute is applied. And on his scales the state's interest preponderates.

The line of analysis seems to me totally uncongenial and verging on the absurd. It in effect tells the Negro that Virginia can curtail seriously the activities of the NAACP because of Virginia's benign interest in protecting Negro clients from the con-

flicts of interest that may arise when they are repre-
sented by NAACP lawyers in civil-rights cases without
financial cost to themselves.

Having said this, let me hasten to repeat that
Justice Harlan is led to such logical extremes by
an almost heroic desire to neutralize litigation on
race issues. He cites impressive authority, at the
state court level, of regulation, in the name of legal
ethics, of reasonably attractive socially conscious
methods of recruiting law business, such as union
reference schemes in personal injury cases.[152] He
wishes to treat this case no differently than any
other; Justice Douglas, on the other hand, wishes
to outlaw the South. Neither approach can be
right, and yet it is a challenge to us all to devise
any third one.

We turn now to the second phase of the attack
which has involved less direct measures and has
centered on efforts to compel disclosure of NAACP
membership. The problem has been before the
Supreme Court five times since 1958, and it is our
purpose now to pass these cases in quick review
and extract from them the major free-speech point
involved.

In three cases the issue has arisen under a state
law seeking to compel the disclosure of NAACP membership lists. The ostensible purpose of the state
law has varied somewhat from case to case, but
each time a unanimous Court has invalidated the

measure. Since history is ironic in these matters
we begin the story with a 1928 case, *Bryant* v.
Zimmerman,[153] which involved disclosure of the
membership list of the Klu Klux Klan. With the
exception of a dissent on jurisdictional grounds by
Justice McReynolds, the court was unanimous in
upholding the measure. The New York statute in
question was limited to "oath bound organizations."
The Court, in an opinion by Justice Van Devanter,
read the law as "proceeding on the theory . . . that
requiring this information to be supplied for the
public files will operate as an effective or substantial
deterrent from violations of public and private right
to which the organization might be tempted if such
a disclosure were not required." The Court also
notes legislative findings that the KKK was dedicated to "white supremacy" and was conducting "a
crusade against Catholics, Negroes, and Jews and
stimulating hurtful religious and race prejudice."
Hence it was permissible to classify it differently
from certain other oath-bound groups which were
exempt under the statute. When the Southern states
turned to compulsory disclosure as a tactic, they,
of course, pointed to the Bryant case. Since white
supremacists had been held subject to such a law,
how could the Court now deny the state the power
to treat Negro activists in a similar way?

The first of the contemporary cases to reach the
Court was *NAACP* v. *Alabama*,[154] decided June

30, 1958. The NAACP had never complied with the Alabama statute requiring a foreign corporation to qualify for doing business in the state by filing its charter and designating an agent for the service of process. In 1956, the state attorney-general brought suit to oust NAACP from the state on the ground that in doing business in the state without complying with the qualification statute, it had caused irreparable injury. The bill in equity mentioned among its activities injurious in Alabama the Montgomery bus boycott and the furnishing of legal assistance to Negro students seeking to enrol in the state universities. In the course of the ouster litigation, the court ordered the NAACP to produce various records including its membership list so that the state could properly prepare for the ouster hearing. The NAACP having refused to furnish the membership list, it was cited for contempt and fined $10,000, the fine to increase to $100,000 if there was not compliance within five days. It was the appeal from the contempt citation which came to the Supreme Court.

In a unanimous opinion by Justice Harlan, the Court reversed the judgment. After first holding that the association has standing to assert rights of non-disclosure which may belong principally to its individual members, the Court firmly holds that such disclosure would violate First Amendment rights. The logic is crisp. First, association with others may be indispensable to "effective advocacy of public and private points of view" and the right to associate for the purpose of group advocacy is as fully protected by the Constitution as is the individual right of advocacy. Secondly, there is a recognized relationship between privacy and freedom of association; if disclosure is compelled here, it will have adverse consequences on the freedom to associate, given the climate of opinion in the South. "We think it apparent," Justice Harlan states, "that compelled disclosure of petitioner's Alabama membership is likely to affect adversely the ability of petitioner and its members to pursue their collective effort to foster beliefs which they admittedly have the right to advocate in that it may induce members to withdraw from the Association and dissuade others from joining it because of fear of exposure of their beliefs shown through their associations and of the consequences of this exposure."[155] Thirdly, this, therefore, is a law applying sanctions to speech and association; and it matters not that the sanction *comes not directly from state action* but from the private community response. It is the state action which has triggered the community response; to borrow a phrase from another corner of the law's web, we can say that the state action in compelling disclosure is the proximate cause of the private social sanction. Fourthly, for this kind of interference with speech the appropriate test of constitutionality is balancing the state interest against the loss of freedom; to meet this test, the state, in a formula originated by Justice Frankfurter in *Sweezy,*[156] must show "a subordinating interest which is compelling"; and finally, the state here utterly fails to show a sufficient interest in obtaining the names of members. The names will have no bearing on the issues in the litigation in which they were requested.

The result is fine, and the Court appears in command of a full-blown theory for handling a new kind of speech problem.[157] We shall return to the theory after looking at the other cases in this sequence.[158] For the moment, three observations are in order. First, the Court is surprisingly inept in distinguishing *Bryant* v. *Zimmerman.* It does so on the ground that the organization there involved had engaged in unlawful actions, and on the ground that the Klan, unlike the NAACP, had totally refused to comply. It seems to me there is a far firmer distinction available. In *Bryant* the disclosure was intended by the state as a method of policing the organization; hence, its legitimacy was to be tested as would be more direct regulation. What poses the dilemma for the modern disclosure case is that it can be argued that the disclosure is for other purposes than regulation of speech and assembly and that the adverse consequences are an unfortunate and unintended by-product of regulation aimed at other ends. Alabama presumably could not directly seek to inhibit membership in the NAACP; New York could presumably inhibit membership in the Klan. The problem in the instant case is whether Alabama, while ostensibly pursuing some other goal, can indirectly, by use of disclosure, inhibit membership in the NAACP.

The second point is simply a cross-reference back to *Beauharnais.* We call attention to the notable difference in the two speech tests Justice Frankfurter has given the world. In *Beauharnais,* whether group libel could be deterred directly and totally by criminal sanction was to be determined by asking whether the statute was "a willful and purposeless regulation unrelated to the welfare of the state." Where, however, as here or in *Sweezy,* the issue is whether speech and association can be indirectly and partially deterred, the test is whether the statute reflects "a subordinating interest of the state that is compelling."

The third point is simply a cross-reference back to Justice Harlan in *Button.* Why does the balance weigh so differently for him in the two cases?

The Court gets its second chance to exercise this line of analysis in *Bates* v. *Little Rock,*[159] decided in February 23, 1960. This time it is Little Rock and a municipal ordinance involving occupational license taxes. In 1957, the ordinance had been amended to ask for certain information "including dues and contributions" and "by whom paid." The announced purpose was that many charitable not-for-profit organizations, as subterfuges for business operated for profit, were avoiding the tax; hence, the information was required of *all* organizations. The NAACP complied with all requests except again the membership list; the local branch did, however, furnish a financial statement for the prior year, an acknowledgment that it was a branch of the national organization, the names of its officers, and a statement of its purposes taken from the original 1909 NAACP charter.

In another unanimous decision, the Court finds the ordinance invalid. This time the majority opinion is by Justice Stewart, and there is a brief separate concurrence by Justices Black and Douglas. The majority opinion reiterates the logic of the Alabama case; there is here the same indirect sanction on freedom of speech and association flowing from the disclosure, and the same test of state interest is appropriate. While recognizing a paramount state interest in matters of taxation, the Court can find no basis on which the state can claim to need the membership identity for its purposes, since the tax is not based on income and since it is obvious on the face of it that the organization is not engaged in activity subject to the tax.

The separate Black-Douglas opinion is apparently meant to reject any balancing once it is recognized that First Amendment rights are involved and are impaired. They state: "We believe that First Amendment rights are beyond abridgement either by legislation that directly restrains their exercise or by suppression or impairment through harassment, humiliation, or exposure by government."[160] This opens a major point to which we shall return.

It might be noted that neither *Alabama* nor *Bates* traps the Court in the dilemmas of realism as did *Button*. The Court can take the state's claim at face value and still find the measure invalid. In fact, the whole enterprise bears a marked resemblance to tax avoidance maneuvers. The state cannot afford to be candid about why it wants disclosure of the names as New York could afford to be in the Bryant case. It therefore seeks some *other* purpose such as the qualification of foreign corporations or the levying of occupational license taxes. While these are purposes admittedly neutral and admittedly within the state's legitimate areas of concern and interest, the fatal difficulty is that the state cannot connect up its need for the names with its avowed purpose in asking for them. The problem of the South, therefore, in this line of cases, is to find a proper purpose for information which it wants for improper purposes.

Apparently the South won't take a clear constitutional no for an answer. In May 22, 1961, the Court decides *Louisiana* v. *NAACP*, a case we have met earlier in our discussion.[161] This time the law

requires certain not-for-profit organizations to file
their membership lists, and happily for Louisiana
the origins of the law are different. It appears it
was passed in 1924 "to curb the Ku Klux Klan."
The opinion of the Court by Justice Douglas is
oddly unsatisfactory; probably the difficulty is that
the case is at a preliminary stage; it is on appeal
from a temporary injunction granted against the
enforcement of the statute, and there will be a full
hearing before the injunction becomes final. This
time the clean logic of the *Alabama* and *Bates*
opinions is missing; and appropriately, Justices
Harlan and Stewart, the authors of those opinions
concur only in the result. In any event, in his brief
opinion Douglas does not rely on *Alabama* and
Bates as disposing of this case, either because at
this early state it is unclear what the state's interest
in disclosure is or, as is more likely, because the
state is alleging its old interest in controlling groups
like the Klan. The opinion, therefore, goes on the
grounds that the end could be "more narrowly
achieved" and that, therefore, the interference with
constitutional freedoms is unnecessary and hence
invalid. The Court relies on *Shelton* v. *Tucker*,[162]
which we are about to discuss and in which this
subtle shift in the logic of handling compulsory disclosure cases emerges as a principal point. Finally,
we should add that Justices Clark and Frankfurter
also concur separately on the basis that the case
will now go back for a full hearing. The slightly

awkward feature in all this is that this is the third time in five years that compulsory disclosure of NAACP membership lists in a Southern state is in issue; and while decision is still unanimous, this time there are four justices who carefully abstain from joining in the majority opinion.

In *Shelton* v. *Tucker,* which the Court decides December 20, 1960, and which involves no mention of the NAACP by name, we have the same problem but in a quite different form. An Arkansas statute enacted in 1958 at a special session of the legislature required as a condition of employment as teacher in any state-supported school or college, the annual filing of an affidavit listing "without limitation" every organization to which the teacher has belonged or made a contribution in the preceding five years. The three petitioners, teachers in the public schools, declining to file the affidavit, sue to enjoin the enforcement of the statute. Each offers a non-communist affidavit, and it is disclosed at the trial that one of the petitioners has been a member of the NAACP. Once again the Supreme Court invalidates the state effort. But this time it is a five to four decision, and there are dissenting opinions by Justices Frankfurter and Harlan.

Here, as in the prior cases, the involuntary disclosure is thought to have some negative consequences for the freedom of association, but the majority opinion by Justice Stewart begins by conceding that *NAACP* v. *Alabama* and *Bates* v. *Little*

Rock do not control the case at bar. "Here by
contrast," says Justice Stewart, "there can be no
question of the relevance of a state's inquiry into
the fitness and competence of its teachers."[163] Does
then this "subordinating interest of the state" dispose of the problem? The answer is "no" because
the inquiry is unnecessarily broad, and, as anticipated in the discussion of *NAACP* v. *Louisiana,* the
case adds a new doctrinal wing to the problem of
speech and disclosure. The formula now is that even
where the state's interest and purpose are legitimate,
and substantial, "that purpose cannot be pursued by
means that broadly stifle fundamental personal liberties when the end can be more narrowly achieved."
The error of the state of Arkansas has been in
asking under compulsion for far more information
from the individual teacher than it needs for its
legitimate purposes. The Court finds precedent for
this means-end formula in several of the prior
street littering cases.[164]

It might be noted that the Stewart opinion does
not specify just what less the state might have asked
to get the information it ostensibly wanted. It might
also be noted that the Court does not even find it
necessary to distinguish *Garner* v. *Board of Public
Works,*[165] decided in 1951. There the Court has held
that the state could compel disclosure by public
employees of whether they had been members of
the Communist Party. In such a situation the state

interest in the loyalty of prospective public employees was viewed as outweighing the negative impact of disclosure on the employees' freedom of association. And under the law in question, the employee was left with the privacy of all other associations but this one.

The state could, of course, cure the evil of breadth found in *Shelton* v. *Tucker* by asking only whether the employee was a member of NAACP. But were it to do so, it would confront the difficulty that it has no legitimate interest in this information as it had in *Garner,* and the *Bates* rule would apply directly.

Thus the Court is once again able to defeat the Southern tactics without violating etiquette by inquiring into the precise motivation for the statute. Yet the law was enacted in a special emergency session in 1958; originally, it will be recalled, there had been the companion statute barring all members of the NAACP from public employment which the federal district court had found invalid in *Shelton* v. *McKinley.*[166] Indeed, the Arkansas legislature had added its own ironic note; section 7 of the statute announced that the school segregation decisions "require the solution of a great variety of local public school problems of considerable complexity immediately," hence making the quest for qualified teachers all the more important.

There is an engaging interplay between three groups of cases here. First, there are the cases like

Shelton v. Tucker in which the interest is legitimate but the inquiry is unnecessarily broad; second, there are cases like Bates in which the inquiry is narrow but the state cannot establish that it has an appropriate interest; finally, there are cases like Bryant and Garner in which the decisive circumstances is the official notice taken of the evil and danger of the particular association which could be regulated directly and, therefore, can be regulated indirectly by disclosure.

The Shelton case awakens greater interest when we turn to the opinions of the dissenters. Taking the state's purposes and motives at face value, as did Justice Stewart, they argue that the Court cannot say the state's inquiry is needlessly broad. Thus they put to us the issue of whether the result of the majority can be reached persuasively if we do not throw into the argument at some point the fact that we all know what the state was really up to; and if it cannot be, are we then allowed to use the nasty fact? Or must we, for the sake of neutrality, permit the state to infringe liberty? Once more we are invited to note the strains these cases put upon a legal system. Once again, the great question is: Can our law accommodate the proper adjudication of such controversies?

Neither Justice Harlan nor Justice Frankfurter in dissent are totally oblivious to the reality here. They would both, however, wait until the discriminatory use of the information became a matter of record and then act. "All that is now here," says Justice Harlan, "is the validity of the statute on its face and I am unable to agree that in this posture of things the enactment can be said to be unconstitutional."[167] And Justice Frankfurter states, after noting there is nothing in the record showing unfair use of the information requested by the state: "It will be time enough if such use is made to hold the application of the statute unconstitutional."[168] The impression is that it will not surprise Justices Harlan and Frankfurter any more than it will the other justices if it should transpire that the sole function of the Arkansas statute is to pounce on and get at teachers who disclose membership in the NAACP. The difference between majority and dissent then lies not so much in the greater realism of the majority as in the greater patience of the dissenters.

The effort of Justice Frankfurter to spell out why the state is not utterly unreasonable in asking for so much information strikes my ear, as did the opinion of Justice Harlan in *Button*, as a singularly unhappy performance. With an ingenuity that reminds one of a sixteenth-century English judge employing the doctrine of *mitior sensus* in defamation,[169] Justice Frankfurter explains:

> Granted that a teacher's membership in the First Street Congregation is standing alone of little relevance to what may be rightly expected of a teacher, is that membership equally irrelevant when it is discovered that the teacher is in fact a

member of the First Street Congregation and the
Second Street Congregation and the Third Street
Congregation and the 4-H Club and the 5-H Club
and half a dozen other groups? [170]

Thus the point is that the school board has an
interest in finding out whether its teachers are com-
mitted to so many organizations that their work
will suffer. And to the obvious rejoinder that if
this is the state's interest it can surely be satisfied
by asking to how many organizations the teacher
belongs and how much time he spends on them, we
are told:

> The answer to such questions could reasonably
> be regarded by a state legislature as insufficient
> . . . because the veracity of the answer is more
> difficult to test in cases where doubts as to veracity
> may arise. . . . [171]

Finally, we are told the broad listing of organizations "may serve the purpose of making known to
school authorities persons who come into contact
with the teacher in all of the phases of his activity
in the community and who can be questioned, if need
be, concerning the teacher's conduct in matters which
this Court can certainly not now say are lacking in
any pertinence to professional fitness." [172]

It is clear, I think, that the technique of balancing
has not yet been perfected as an analytic tool; it
appears to change from case to case. Whereas the
test had been "a subordinating interest of the state
which was compelling," the test now in the hands

of Justices Frankfurter and Harlan seems to be
that any interest of the state, however trivial, out-
weighs any consequential interference with speech
or assembly, however substantial. And while in
the earlier cases the Court had been perceptive and
eloquent about the dangers of exposure of membership in the NAACP, in *Shelton* they refer to the
negative consequences of disclosure only incidentally.

Shelton thus emerges as a surprisingly awkward
case to dispose of. Perhaps the difficulty is this: the
court, while steadfastly protecting membership in
the NAACP against disclosure, has not by any means
gone so far as to accord to it the status of a constitutionally inviolate privacy, such as might perhaps
today be given to the way one votes. The result is
that on current doctrine NAACP privacy will be protected only so long as the state cannot find some half-
way sensible reason for invading it. If Arkansas
can devise some more precise way of asking teachers,
including those who do belong to the NAACP, to disclose their organizations, there is nothing in *Shelton*
v. *Tucker* that will bar the inquiry whatever its
impact on the vitality of the NAACP.

It was inevitable that the South, in its pursuit of
NAACP membership, should use the device which had
been a main feature of the anti-communist decade—
the legislative investigating committee. In *Gibson*
v. *Florida Legislative Investigation Committee*,[173]
decided March 25, 1963, the disclosure problem
came to the court in this form. *Gibson,* which will

bring this segment of our discussion to a close, is worthy of a lecture in its own right; it intersects with the special and complex history of doctrines developed for the investigating committee;[174] it produces the widest spectrum of opinions in the Court with Justices Black and Douglas in separate concurring opinions falling on one side of the majority opinion of Justice Goldberg, and Justices Harlan and White in dissent falling on the other side. It is not easy to say whether the *Gibson* decision is a sport born of the pressures of the moment and destined to be limited to its special facts or whether it will become the germinal precedent on the investigative committee in the same fashion the *New York Times* case, discussed in the preceding lecture, may become the germinal precedent for new free-speech theory.

Before turning to the case, a very brief word about the history of law and investigative committees may prove helpful. The committee, after a slow legal start in the last century, was strongly underwritten in *McGrain v. Daugherty*[175] in 1927, a case involving the once famous Teapot Dome Scandal. From then on, through the heyday of the House Un-American Activities Committee and the McCarthy Committee, legislative investigation seemed for all practical purposes omnipotent and beyond judicial reach. Then, in 1957, the Supreme Court in two cases, *Watkins*[176] and *Sweezy,*[177] gave brief promise of vigorous judicial review of investigations. But by 1960, a further series of important cases, *Barenblatt*,[178] *Uphaus*,[179] *Wilkinson*,[180] and *Braden*,[181] all of which upheld the investigative power, again suggested that a court can not devise doctrine which can limit investigations. *Gibson* is the latest Supreme Court decision in this sequence and its denial of committee power may require a major reappraisal of the law on this highly important American political institution.

Until *Gibson,* there had been three main lines of challenge to committees: (1) that they lacked genuine legislative purpose and were being used as a new kind of sanction, or a bastard form of trial; (2) that in certain areas their use and their efforts at compulsory disclosure violated First Amendment rights; and finally, (3) that, more technically and narrowly, the particular question asked was not pertinent to the inquiry they were authorized by the parent legislature to make. Although the first two grounds sparked increasingly eloquent dissenting opinions,[182] it was only the pertinency grounds which commanded majority support.[183] Lack of pertinency, however, proved a slender reed on which to rest,[184] and a careful committee could always by explicit statement succeed in connecting its question with the topic of its inquiry.

In capsule form this is almost the whole doctrinal story up to the *Gibson* decision. I say almost because there are two other trends in the recent opinions, both of which appear to harden into new doctrine in *Gibson.* First, in *Barenblatt,* Justice Harlan, for the majority, dropped a casual dictum in support of the fact that the inquiry presented no specially offensive features. It did not pillory the witness. "Nor," he adds, "did petitioner's appearance as a witness follow from indiscriminate dragnet procedures lacking in probable cause for belief that he possessed information which might be helpful to the committee."[185] The sentence is repeated verbatim in Justice Stewart's opinion for the majority in *Wilkinson;* and in that case, counsel for the committee, in explaining to the witness the pertinency of the question he was about to ask him, speaks of "laying a foundation."[186] Finally, in his dissent in *Braden,* Justice Douglas complains that "no foundation was ever laid" for asking Braden about communist affiliation.[187] We cannot be sure what these phrases mean, but they are highly reminiscent of Fourth Amendment concepts; the idea seems to be that there must be "probable cause" for "searching and seizing" the witness by summoning him to the investigation.

The other trend comes from the Uphaus case which has considerable similarity to *Gibson* on its facts. Here the New Hampshire attorney-general investigating subversion in the state as a one-man committee asked Uphaus as executive director of a group called World Fellowship, Inc., for its membership list. Uphaus refused, and the Court upheld a contempt conviction. By this time *NAACP* v. *Alabama* had been decided, and the majority sought to meet its requirement of some "compelling" state interest justifying the interference with associational privacy. The avowed interest put forth by the state was control of subversion. The Court, to meet the Alabama test, had to connect this interest up with the membership information they were seeking from Uphaus. They did so on the grounds that the attorney-general had information tending to show that the organization might harbor subversive persons. And the Court spoke of the "nexus" between World Fellowship and subversive activities.[188]

These three terms, "laying a foundation," "probable cause," and "nexus," are thus available to the Court in *Gibson;* and whether they mean the same thing or not, the Court attempts to mold them into a single doctrine.

On its facts, the Gibson case presents an interesting variant on *all* of the prior subversion cases and on *all* the prior NAACP cases. As the inquiry was finally narrowed by the Florida Supreme Court, the witness was asked whether certain individuals, allegedly communists, were members of the NAACP. The situation is thus different from that in the subversion cases, since here the question is not whether the witness or certain other people are

Communists; the question assumes that. Nor is it like the other NAACP cases, since only this very limited information about membership is requested and since a very specific purpose is given for requesting it. The case is thus at once an inquiry into subversion and a request for NAACP membership.

There is *one further oddity* about the fact situation. The defendant is willing to testify from memory, if he can, as to whether the individuals in question are members of the NAACP; it turns out he cannot, and the committee then requests that he bring his records simply to refresh his memory. It is his refusal to bring the records with him to refresh his memory that precipitates the contempt. Insofar as we are concerned with the decision in the precise case before the Court, it must be admitted that this circumstance spoils the case, so to speak. Justice Harlan in dissent effectively utilizes this aspect of the case suggesting wryly that the Court was protecting the witness's right to give "only partial and inaccurate testimony."[189] Justice Goldberg, for the majority, does not refer to the problem, and as a result his interesting and perhaps important rationale for the decision is somewhat impeached.

At the outset of his opinion, Justice Goldberg notes the happy circumstance that both sides agree on the "proper test" for a case of this sort. He then quotes the committee's brief to the effect that "the case hinges entirely on the question of whether the evidence before the Committee was . . . sufficient to show probable cause or nexus between the NAACP Miami Branch and Communist activities."[190] The Court then restates this by adding the term "foundation," so that we now have the three ideas marching together. Armed with this test, the majority then proceeds to examine in detail the evidence before the committee and concludes that no sufficient connection between the NAACP and communist activities has been shown. "An adequate foundation for the inquiry must be laid. . . . No such foundation has been laid here."[191] It follows, therefore, that the inquiry was into a constitutionally privileged area and that the committee had no power to compel an answer.

Despite the force and apparent clarity of the majority view, as soon as we turn to the dissents we realize that confusion reigns. Justice White, as I read him, appears to think that, given the test, there was sufficient evidence before the committee to justify the inquiry. Justice Harlan, as I read him, challenges whether this is after all the "proper test."

At this point we must pause for analytic refreshment. There are at least two subtly different ideas involved in the Gibson situation. There is the general premise on which all are in agreement that compulsory disclosure of membership may have negative consequences on the freedom of associa-

tion and that these must be confronted in weighing
whether a given inquiry is proper. However, at this
point there are two related but different approaches
percolating in the opinions in *Gibson*. First, there
is the idea of *Alabama* and *Bates* that the state
must offer some good reason for needing the information; the requests in those cases failed, it will be
recalled, because the court could see no connection
between qualifying an out-of-state corporation or
administering an occupational license tax *and* the
membership list of the NAACP. Secondly, there is
the idea, apparently borrowed from the Fourth
Amendment, that invasions of privacy have to be
limited to those with some likelihood of success;
dragnets are unnecessarily and offensively imprecise.

The Braden case can be used to illustrate what
the difference is here. Braden was asked whether
he was a Communist at the time of certain activity
in the South. Under the first test, since the committee was inquiring into subversion in the South,
information whether Braden was a Communist
would arguably be useful to it. And this was the
view of the Court in the Braden case in subordinating Braden's interest in privacy to the state's
interest in subversion. The second test, however,
is illustrated by Douglas's dissent in *Braden*. He
complained that there was no foundation laid for
asking Braden that question; without the foundation, the summoning of Braden was an unlawful

invasion of his privacy. To put all this one other way: under the first notion, the problem is not whether the witness has the information but whether the information will be useful and relevant to the professed state purpose; under the second test, the problem is not whether the information will be useful and relevant but whether there is sufficient reason for thinking the witness has the information.

In *Gibson* the situation is complex. Since the state is studying Communist infiltration into lawful organizations, the information that alleged Communists are members of the NAACP will be arguably useful to it, and the witness as president of the local branch will have that information. Hence, the first test is satisfied. However, there must be some reason for asking the NAACP the question instead of, for example, the Miami branch of the Republican party. It is here that a foundation, a nexus, a probable cause must be shown. And it would fail, it should be noted, either because there might be no basis shown for believing that the alleged Communists are Communists or because there might be no basis shown for believing they have any role in the NAACP. What divides the Court in *Gibson* then is twofold: (1) Is the second test an improper test? And (2) under it was a sufficient foundation laid in *Gibson?* Justice Goldberg says no to both questions; Justice White says yes to the second; Justice Harlan says yes to the first.

The majority opinion is less helpful than it might be in this impasse. It does not clearly distinguish between the two tests; it relies too much on the concession of counsel and hence does not establish that the second test is proper. Similarly, Justice Harlan, in an exceptionally able dissent, does not appear to recognize that the majority is attempting to follow his own dictum about dragnets in *Barenblatt*.

There is still another important point to make about these two tests. They are responsive to different evils of the investigative committee process and to different notions of privacy. The first test is designed to protect anonymity and privacy from disclosure, that is, from the compulsion to answer the question. The second test, however, is designed to protect the citizen from being bothered, from having his daily privacy upset by governmental action; its purpose is to protect the witness from being summoned and asked the question. And if it is thought that this is an oddly trivial interest to treat so solemnly, the answer is to look to the Fourth Amendment.

Gibson thus has within it the germs of a major development of law in this area of investigative committees. The majority opinion does not, however, quite satisfy, because Justice Goldberg is not sufficiently aware of how good and powerful an idea he is playing with. I am troubled by Justice

Harlan's apparently deadly quip that the announced rule and its "nexus" criterion "require an investigating agency to prove in advance the very things it is trying to find out."[192] Is it a proper answer here to say that the same point might be made about requiring the government to arrest only people it "knows" are guilty or only seek evidence it "knows" is there? Can the Fourth Amendment be imported in this fashion into the First? I must confess I am not sure.

The novelty and daring of the majority approach in *Gibson* is illustrated not so much by the test they announce as it is by the seriousness with which they apply it. There is, after all, "foundation" testimony before the Florida committee. The committee investigator testifies that the fourteen persons in issue were or had been Communists or members of fronts and had been members or participated in the affairs of the NAACP branch. Justice Goldberg now becomes the logician[193] and meticulously weighs the testimony, finding it wanting. Several of the fourteen are no longer residents of Florida; it is unclear whether any of the others were members or whether their participation consisted simply in attending NAACP meetings open to the public; it is not clear that any of the fourteen was ever in an influential position in the organization; nor is it clear that their alleged communist affiliations and their alleged NAACP associations coincided in time.

On so ambiguous a showing Justice Goldberg declines, in effect, to issue the search warrant. If the threshold for investigative intrusion is to be set this high, surely both *Braden* and *Uphaus* have become insupportable precedents.

There is one further observation invited by this collision of views between Justices Harlan and Goldberg. We are meeting once again the issue of judicial realism. How seriously is the Court to take a Southern claim that the NAACP has been infiltrated to some degree by subversives and that it is the South's duty to protect the NAACP from Communist capture? No one talks to the point, but Justice Goldberg's unusually careful scrutiny of the foundation may well be in silent response to it.

The interactions and interrelationships between the majority opinion of Justice Goldberg and those of Justices Harlan and White in dissent are thus complex and rich with significance. But there is still another segment to the dizzy doctrinal ballet generated by the Gibson case. We still have Justices Black and Douglas to hear from. Although, as we have seen, the majority opinion might well impose unprecedentedly stringent limits on investigative inquiry, Justices Black and Douglas, apparently distrustful of the probable cause criterion, seek firmer and higher ground.

The very brief concurring opinion of Justice Black is, I gather, intended to assert again the position that even in disclosure cases where the impact of the sanction on freedoms of speech and association is indirect and consequential, the state has no power to generate such by-product abridgement. "Since, as I believe, the National Association of Colored People and its members have a constitutional right to choose their own associates, I cannot understand by what constitutional authority Florida can compel answers to questions which abridge that right."[194]

Justice Douglas, however, uses the occasion for an unusually elaborate and eloquent opinion in which he rejects the probable cause analysis of his own dissenting opinion in *Braden* and now offers a new approach to both the privacy of organizations and beliefs and to the limiting of legislative investigatory power. The thesis echoes one which had been advanced unsuccessfully in the late forties against the House Un-American Activities Committee. The thesis is that power to investigate for a legislative committee depends entirely on the power to legislate. The key premise then is: "When the State or Federal Government is prohibited from dealing with a subject, it has no constitutional privilege to investigate it."[195] Freedom of association is given an inviolate privacy by the First Amendment; hence, questions inquiring into membership, whatever their purpose, transgress constitutional limits. "In sum the State and Federal Governments, by force of the First Amendment, are barred from investigating any person's faith or ideology by summoning him or summoning officers or members of his society, church or club."[196]

The position, although yielding the same results, is subtly different from that of Justice Black. As I read Justice Black, he is saying that disclosure, by the social pressures it may generate, is itself a sanction; hence, use of it abridges freedom of speech and association; and any abridgement of these freedoms, direct or indirect, intended or inadvertent, on the part of the state is prohibited by the First Amendment; therefore, disclosure of membership cannot be compelled. Justice Douglas, on the other hand, puts his emphasis on privacy as the key value; there are in the society islands of privacy which the government may not touch; association is one of these; hence, the disclosure of membership cannot be compelled. In this large form, as he well recognizes, he is calling for a considerable revamping of the law on investigations. He advances in the course of his analysis, however, an effective point specific to the case at hand; he can see no limit to the invasions of privacy that follow from the logic of the Harlan and White opinions. "If the files of the NAACP can be ransacked because some Communists may have joined it, then all walls of privacy are broken down. By that reasoning the records of the confessional can be ransacked because a 'subversive' or criminal was implicated." [197]

In the end, *Gibson* yields *five* neatly different positions on the legal rules for review of investigative committees, indicating again, if any further evidence were needed, that the legal issues raised by this important and troublesome American institution are stubborn indeed. In the middle we have the position of the majority that some reasonable basis for troubling the particular witness must be established, at least in areas which are sensitive— the touchstone here it seems to me, although the Court has yet to say so, is Fourth Amendment policy. Then we have the position of Justice White which would apparently subscribe to this requirement but would not scrutinize very carefully the "foundation" if any was offered. Third, there is the position of Justice Harlan which would limit inquiry only by the substantiality of the state's interest and by the relevance to it of the information sought; that is, he would get his criteria solely from *Alabama* and *Bates* and would not add a probable cause condition. Then, to the left of the majority opinion, we have Justices Black and Douglas both arguing that the rule is too narrow and that more absolute protection is needed. Justice Black would therefore bar all consequential abridgements resulting from disclosure with the same firmness he would bar abridgements resulting from direct use of criminal sanctions. Finally, there is Justice Douglas who would create certain islands of inviolate privacy in the society which a committee could not invade by investigative process.

As a sort of epilogue to this long story I would add a few words on the celebrated controversy over balancing and the First Amendment.[198] We have seen that cases involving compulsory disclosure have raised First Amendment issues very different from the classic ones of seditious libel. As we move from *Bryant* to *Bates* to *Shelton* to *Gibson,* we sense the Court evolving varying approaches to restrict such inquiries. The NAACP and its enemies have made great contributions to the law in this area in the past decade, and it is clear that the story is not yet fully told. But a number of significant points have emerged. First, we are never sure whether it is privacy or freedom of speech and association that is being protected, or whether these are two ways of saying the same thing. In any event, the Court has been notably explicit about recognizing that disclosure may become a sanction in a hostile community and that freedom may require anonymity.[199] There are interesting behavioral assumptions in this logic, and it is not the least of the NAACP's values that it has made it possible for us to have a genuine instance in which disclosure of member- ship in a *lawful* group may have highly negative consequences. Further, *Shelton* and *Gibson* have suggested approaches to the problem via privacy echoing policies of the Fourth rather than the First Amendment.

Secondly, it would seem to me helpful to distinguish between the intended use of disclosure as a sanction, as in *Bryant,* and the inadvertent use, as ostensibly in the other cases.

Thirdly, it is, I think, only in this category of officially unintended consequences of disclosure that the balancing controversy has, in fact, arisen insofar as it relates to decisions. Unfortunately, it has evoked a rhetoric far broader than its problem and has put in philosophic issue the whole enterprise of judicial review.

My fourth and final word is this: These cases present an unresolved problem for First Amendment theory. It is abundantly clear that one cannot approach them via a clear and present danger formula. Balancing seems to me a slippery and ambiguous enterprise for the judiciary. Yet, I do not quickly see how one can agree with Justice Black that even inadvertent interference with free speech and free association coming as a by-product of otherwise proper official action must be categorically prohibited as an abridgement of these First Amendment freedoms. In brief, I'm stuck.

III

Trespass and the First Amendment

IN THIS LECTURE we shift to still a third sector of
First Amendment theory. And once again our
problems find their roots in distinctive aspects of the
contemporary Negro protest. The nature and tex-
ture of our discussion will change considerably, however. In the first two lectures we were running,
albeit a little breathlessly, along with the rapidly
moving legal developments of the moment. Here
we are going to try to run a little ahead of them.
We are, that is, going to put ourselves a problem
suggested by some of the recent cases and quite
possibly deeply involved in the sit-in cases.[200] You
are free to regard the message in this lecture,
although it may have some practical utility, as primarily an academic fantasy, a playful effort to look
at certain familiar ideas in a new way.

In the last lecture we were largely concerned with
the Negro movement in the courts, with the mass
effort to compel by litigation redress of Negro
grievances, and with the role of the NAACP as the

mobilizer of legal attack. Here we pick up the great change in the Negro movement which has occurred in the last two or three years. The Negro protest has moved from the courts into the streets. It has become a massive self-help movement. You are all familiar from the daily headlines with the general flavor of the tactics involved—the March to Washington, the bus boycott, the school boycotts, and, above all, the sit-ins. The protest so far has been imaginative, tactful, effective, and the news story of the decade.

This phenomenon is rich in significance. Indeed, it may prove to work better for the Negro, and for the country, than the "all deliberate speed" of the courts. It has given the Negro a sense of pride, of hope, and of vitality. It has accelerated remarkably the development of Negro leadership. It has the muscle tone of revolution. Yet thus far it has been executed with an astonishing sense of tact and legality.[201] It has often seemed to me to be the first revolution in history conducted, so to speak, on advice of counsel. Whether the movement will be able to control the forces and energies it so ably generates only the future can tell. But, in any event, the massive self-help tactic has put large questions to the law. It should be emphasized that what the Negro needs from the law in this instance is simply to be let alone. He needs, that is, to put it technically, to have his self-help measures privileged. The idea

of self-help is, of course, an old one in law.²⁰² There
are the classic privileges of self-defense and defense
of person; and the history of the labor movement
over the century has been largely the history of the
use of the self-help tactics of strike, boycott, and
picket line. Setting the legal limits to the Negro
use of self-help is one of the great legal issues of
our day.

We do not aspire to deal with the whole of this
issue, but only with what might be called its First
Amendment aspects. Our story begins with the
great sit-in case of 1961, *Garner* v. *Louisiana*.²⁰³ A
group of Negroes were convicted under a Louisiana
breach of peace statute for sitting-in at lunch counters in a department store, a drug store, and a bus
terminal. All three establishments were open to the
public, had some Negro clientele, but had segregated
lunch counters. The Supreme Court in a unanimous decision upset the convictions. Despite the
unanimity of the result, the case exhibited a wide
variety of approaches, with Justices Frankfurter,
Douglas, and Harlan each writing separate concurring opinions to add to the majority opinion by
the Chief Justice. The case had obviously put a
considerable strain on legal doctrine and gave
promise of future cases which would be even more
troublesome to handle.

For our present purposes, the doctrinal differences
in the opinions can be quickly skimmed. The state

had proceeded under a breach of peace statute. The
Chief Justice, being extremely careful to decide no
more than was absolutely necessary to upset the
convictions, held that there was simply no evidence
in the record to support the conclusion that the
peaceful sitting at the counters by the defendants
was a breach of peace even if the crime were defined
so as to include conduct which, although overtly
peaceful, carried the likelihood of imminent violence. Hence, the convictions violated procedural due
process. Justice Frankfurter concurred on the same
ground, explicitly negating the possibility of taking
judicial notice of the threat of violence in the explosive context of the sit-in in the South.

There are several things to note about this
approach, which enlisted the support of a majority
of seven on the Court: (1) it is supremely neutral
and applies a rule that has nothing to do with the
race issues as such; it says that in the conviction of
these defendants for this crime the state must, as
in all other criminal cases, satisfy procedural due
process by offering at least some evidence.[204] (2) To
apply this rule the court must ignore the factual
reality which made violence not unlikely and insist
that such matters be offered in proof at the trial
with the opportunity for rebuttal. The case thus
presents once again our perennial issue of the limits
of judicial realism, although this time we have
Justices Douglas and Harlan joining as the two

realists, an unlikely alliance. And (3) the court is able to upset the convictions only because the state has proceeded under a breach of peace statute and not under a criminal trespass statute. The peaceful staying on the property of another without his consent would be adequate evidence of a criminal trespass under a properly drawn statute. Hence the majority has chosen deliberately a very narrow grounds sufficient simply to dispose of the exact case before them but obviously not adequate for the general problem of protecting the sit-in.

Presumably it is this latter consideration that moves Justice Douglas, in a separate concurrence, to a major creative effort to try to establish that the defendants had a constitutional right to be where they were and that the segregation of the lunch counters was unconstitutional action. He argues that it was in response to a coercive state custom which has the force of law and hence represents unconstitutional state action. He further argues that, under state law which licenses them, restaurants become property affected with a public interest and hence cannot segregate. The free-wheeling effort of Justice Douglas to avoid the limitations on private action set up by the architectonic precedent of the Civil Rights cases of 1883[205] did not win the support of any of his judicial colleagues; it is, however, directly responsive to the race issue involved in the case; and it would

moreover be equally available to invalidate a conviction under a criminal trespass statute.[206]

We skip for the moment the opinion of Justice
Harlan, which is to supply our principal theme for
this lecture, to note the fate thus far of the further
sit-in cases that have come to the Court.[207] In June,
1962, in *Taylor* v. *Louisiana*,[208] the Court disposed
of another breach of peace conviction, this time for
a sit-in in the waiting room of a bus terminal. Once
again the Court used the *Garner* rationale of an
utter absence of evidence, noting that the only evidence of unrest came from the violation of a local
custom of segregation, which violated the law where
interstate facilities were involved. In May, 1963,
the Court disposed of three further efforts by
the South to prohibit the sit-ins, *Shuttlesworth*,[209]
Peterson,[210] and *Lombard*.[211] With an ineptness that
is almost amusing, the South fails three more times
to get the pure criminal trespass issue to the Court.
In *Peterson* there is the right form of trespass
statute, but it turns out that the lunch counter is
segregated pursuant to a city ordinance. Hence the
conviction falls. In *Lombard*, the fatal flaw is that
there were public announcements by the mayor and
police chief urging segregation, which are taken to
be sufficient gestures of state action to again render
the segregation on behalf of which the trespass
sanction is sought unconstitutional. In *Shuttlesworth* the defendants are simply charged with incit-

ing the violation of the trespass ordinance; since the crime itself cannot stand constitutionally, neither can a conviction for inciting it. And, finally, since the fall term, a whole new batch of sit-in cases have been argued before the Court. In at least some of these, too, insofar as one can tell from the briefs, it appears that there is again a flaw in the trespass theory: the statutes invoked do not cover refusals to leave after lawful entry.[212] It is thus possible that the Court may once again be able to escape its dilemma on technical grounds. It is possible also that the pending federal civil-rights legislation may make the practical problem obsolete. But there is at the moment a not inconsiderable likelihood that the Court may have to confront the problem of the sit-in under the pure criminal trespass statute. Unless then it is to render this key form of Negro self-help illegal, it will have to break some new ground.

There are not so many possibilities, and it is in this connection that the solution suggested by Justice Harlan in *Garner* may take on significance; and whether it points to a practical solution or not, it provides us with our topic and an engaging First Amendment theme for the remainder of this discussion.

Like Justice Douglas, Justice Harlan is unable to accept the view of the majority in *Garner* that the state court could not take judicial notice of the possibility of violence; there is, therefore, sufficient evidence to support the conviction if it is otherwise supportable. Unwilling to accept the Douglas approaches, Justice Harlan forges a new one of his own. His view merits a full quotation:

> There was more to the conduct of those petitioners than a bare desire to remain at the "white" lunch counter and their refusal of a police request to move from the counter. We would surely have to be blind not to recognize that these petitioners were sitting at those counters where they knew they would not be served, in order to demonstrate that their race was being segregated in dining facilities in this part of the country.
> Such a demonstration in the circumstances . . . is as much a part of the free trade in ideas *Abrams* v. *United States* . . . as is verbal expression more commonly thought of as speech. It, like speech, appeals to good sense and to the power of reason as applied through public discussion, *Whitney* v. *California* . . . just as much as, if not more than, a public oration delivered from a soapbox at a street corner. This Court has never limited the right to speak, a protected liberty under the Fourteenth Amendment . . . to mere verbal expression. [Citing *Stromberg, Thornhill,* and *Barnette* and noting also *NAACP* v. *Alabama.*] If the act of displaying a red flag as a symbol of opposition to organized government is a liberty encompassed within free speech as protected by the Fourteenth Amendment . . . the act of sitting at a privately owned lunch counter with the consent of the owner,[213] as a demonstration of opposition to enforced segregation is surely within the

same range of protections. This is not to say of
course that the Fourteenth Amendment reaches
to demonstrations conducted on private property
over the objection of the owner . . . just as it
would surely not encompass verbal expression in
a private home if the owner has not consented.²¹⁴

This passage seems to me extraordinary in several
respects. First, it quite deliberately associates the
sit-in as a form of communication with the pas-
sionate free-speech rhetoric of Holmes in *Abrams*
and Brandeis in *Whitney*. Indeed, the identification
of the sit-in with a First Amendment freedom could
hardly be more vigorous: "We would surely have
to be blind not to recognize. . . . " Secondly the
statement, with all due respect, comes from an unexpected quarter. If so daring a move was to be made
by the Court, one would not think Justice Harlan
the justice most likely to make it; and ironically he
does not, at least in this instance, get any endorsement from the expected sources, the Chief Justice,
or Justices Brennan, Black, or Douglas. Thirdly,
on the basis of this speech premise, Justice Harlan
is then able to dispose of the case. But he does so,
not directly on the grounds that the state statute
penalizing such sit-in speech abridges speech, but
rather by reliance on *Cantwell* v. *Connecticut*²¹⁵ and
the principle that so general and indiscriminate a
rubric as breach of peace cannot be used in such a
sensitive area. The legislature, we are told, must

focus on the "otherwise protected conduct it is prohibiting and then make a legislative judgment as to
whether that conduct presents so clear and present
a danger to the welfare of the community that it
may legitimately be proscribed."[216] The life of the
law can be full of surprises. One does not, as we
noted in the first lecture, hear much about clear and
present danger these days under any circumstances;
it is amazing to find the formula so seriously used
in a case involving a sit-in.

Our remaining agenda is now set. We wish to
look at a range of problems suggested by the perception of Negro self-help as a speech activity; and,
more particularly, we wish to try our hand at push-
ing the Harlan thesis past the owner-consent point;
did he perhaps make a more generous point than
he aspired to? What, we ask, is the relationship
between trespass and the First Amendment?

Justice Harlan's opinion thus strikes me as a
venture rich in imaginative daring. Yet we cannot
but wonder why he wrote it. For he is carefully
explicit to tell us that he would employ his new
approach only in cases in which the owner of the
private property has not withdrawn his consent to
the presence of the sit-ins. It is difficult to believe
we will ever see another sit-in case in which there
is any ambiguity about the withdrawal of consent.
Justice Harlan, therefore, has launched an exciting,
expansive, new concept for which there will never,
on his view, be another case in which its use will

be appropriate. He has given us a sort of legal version of "The Short Happy Life of Francis Macomber."

As a sociological perception, it seems to me Justice Harlan's characterization of the protest as a First Amendment activity rings true. Certainly the sit-in ceremony, and the South's response to it, have been sensationally successful in making the Negro grievance known, not simply to the Negro community, but to the entire country. And not so much known as felt. The rhetoric of the silent waiting has been extraordinarily good; there cannot be ways of making the point as well with words; and finally, to borrow a point the Court has been eloquent about in leaflet cases, we have again here a problem of the poor man's printing press. The sit-in gesture gives a powerful resource to the Negro community, which does not have great communication resources. In the end, the wisdom and restraint that has, by and large thus far, held the Negro self-help tactic to these gestures of passive, patient, peaceful protest has not only been effective rhetoric but has been the circumstance making it possible and plausible to characterize it as First Amendment activity. Political assassination is a gesture of protest, too, but no one is disposed to work up any First Amendment enthusiasm for it.

At the outset of any effort to treat Negro protest as free speech, we must confront the analogy to picketing. Admittedly it is somewhat unnerving for our enterprise. No one today is happy over the legal career of picketing as free speech. After the first flush of enthusiasm for the metaphor in *Thornhill* v. *Alabama*,[217] in 1940, the Supreme Court seemed devoted to withdrawing its endorsement inch by inch until *International Teamsters* v. *Vogt*,[218] in 1957. Here Justice Frankfurter, speaking for the majority, elaborately reviews the cases after *Thornhill* in which state bans on peaceful picketing have been upheld. He concludes that picketing is speech plus and that various considerations of state policy can provide a basis for regulating the "plus." The result is that under a series of rules keyed to the competitive tort aspects of picketing as activity, the state is about as free to regulate it today as it would have been had the free-speech metaphor never been employed in *Thornhill*. And the demise of the metaphor is marked by the dissent of Justice Douglas in which Justice Black and the Chief Justice join. Justice Douglas speaks of the "retreat" from *Thornhill* becoming a "rout" and says of the present case, "Today the Court signs the formal surrender."[219]

What does the ill-starred history of the identification of picketing with free speech presage for the Negro tactic?[220] It cannot be denied that, like picketing, it is also speech plus, carrying an ambiguous hint of coercion and economic pressure. And, in two respects, it is at a disadvantage in the comparison to picketing. It often takes place on private property, whereas the labor picketing was a use of the streets. Furthermore, whereas mass picketing has been generally disfavored, the Negro tactic very often involves mass behavior. Yet there are some subtle differences between these two forms of symbolic behavior. The Negro protest is directed at the general public, and the grievance which the Negro is airing has constitutional status. Then, too, the behavior is itself different and does not present the special inhibitions of crossing a picket line. But admittedly the picketing analogy presses heavily. Perhaps the best evidence that there are meaningful differences between the labor and the Negro protest is found in the reaction of Justice Harlan. He is very clear in *Button* that litigation is speech plus and thus to be treated differently than is pure speech.[221] He is surely also familiar with the demise of the *Thornhill* doctrine. Yet in *Garner,* he is willing to say, "Such a demonstration in the circumstances is as much a part of the free trade in ideas . . . as is verbal expression. . . . It appeals to the power of reason as applied through public discussion . . . just as much, if not more than, a public oration delivered from a soapbox." So much then for the picketing analogy.

Coming into First Amendment theory from this angle brings us to a body of law largely created by the indefatigable efforts of the Jehovah Witnesses to distribute their pamphlets and play their records. Indeed, it would not be a bad summary of the

last three decades of First Amendment issues
in the Court to say simply: Jehovah Witnesses,
Communists, Negroes.

It will be helpful in the review that follows to
distinguish between the public forum and the private forum. We begin with the public forum, that
is, the streets, the parks, the public halls. The
Negro movement also lays claim to this forum, and
here the problems have been reasonably well worked
out in advance of any special impetus from the
Negro movement. There are perhaps four points
to consider. First, there is the recognition of the
claim to commandeer the public forum, the public
rostrum. The important precedents here are *Davis*
v. *Massachusetts*[222] in 1897 and *Hague* v. *CIO*[223] in
1939. There is a critical shift in theory, if not in
decision, that occurs between these two cases. In
Davis, the defendant was convicted for making a
speech in the Boston Common without first securing
a permit from the mayor as required by ordinance.
The Supreme Judicial Court of Massachusetts in a
decision by Justice Holmes upheld the ordinance and
the conviction, and the United States Supreme Court
affirmed in an opinion by Chief Justice White which
pretty much endorsed the Holmes' opinion. The case
might have been decided on narrow grounds as
the ordinance was directed generally at use of the
Common and not at speech as such; thus it also
dealt with those who would "discharge any cannon

or firearm, expose for sale any goods, wares, or merchandise, erect or maintain any booth, stand, tent, or apparatus for purposes of public amusement." Justice Holmes, in what has become one of his less admired efforts, placed the result, however, on very broad grounds. The legislature as representative of the public, he tells us, has plenary power to regulate the public use of such public property. He then utters a sentence which is deeply ironic in the context of our present effort: "For the Legislature absolutely or conditionally to forbid public speaking in a highway or public park is no more an infringement of the rights of a member of the public than for the owner of a private house to forbid it in his house."[224] Our objective in this lecture is to see if we can turn that sentence upside down.

The United States Supreme Court in its handling of the problem added, if anything, to the breadth of power left the state to control speaking in a public park. Chief Justice White rejected any argument that the control must not be arbitrary. The right to exclude altogether having been established, he argued a familiar White syllogism:

> The right to absolutely exclude all right to use, necessarily includes the authority to determine under what circumstances such use may be availed of, as the greater power contains the lesser.[225]

The issue comes back to the Court forty years later in the Hague case. Among the various griev-

ances therein alleged was the threatened enforcement of an ordinance requiring a permit from the
director of public safety for the holding of any
public assembly on public property. The director,
in turn, was authorized to refuse the permit only
for the purpose of preventing riots, disturbances, or
disorderly assemblage. The ordinance thus differed
from that in the Davis case in that it was directed
only at speech and assembly, and further, there
were allegations of discriminatory enforcement. The
Court speaking through Justice Roberts had, therefore, little difficulty in distinguishing *Davis,* on its
facts, but what is important for our purposes is
the breadth of the new rationale.

Counsel for the city, relying on *Davis,* had con-
tended that "the city's ownership of streets and
parks is as absolute as one's ownership of his home."
Justice Roberts in reply has this to say:

> Wherever the title of streets and parks may
> rest, they have immemorially been held in trust
> for the use of the public and time out of mind
> have been used for the purposes of assembly,
> communicating thoughts between citizens and dis-
> cussing public questions. Such use of the streets
> and public places has from ancient times been
> a part of the privileges, immunities, rights and
> liberties of citizens.[226]

The second point about the public forum is illustrated by the important precedent in *Cox* v. *New*

Hampshire,[227] which holds that although parades are a form of expression, a state may validly require that they be licensed if the licensing scheme is keyed to avoiding traffic problems. The general principle here is one which Alexander Meiklejohn explains in terms of Robert's *Rules of Order;* that is, non-content control of the orderly procedures of speech, a control which on no theory can be regarded as an abridgment of free speech.[228]

The third point is found in three cases decided on the same day in 1951: *Feiner*,[229] *Kunz*,[230] and *Niemotko*.[231] *Feiner,* in the teeth of a very sharp dissent by Justice Black, held that the use of the streets as a forum was limited by notions of breach of peace. Given the circumstances of the particular record, the Supreme Court would not upset the judgment of the police "faced with a crisis." *Kunz* and *Niemotko* both dealt with prior licensing of the use of public forums; in each case the licensing scheme was found invalid because the discretion of the administrative official in the sensitive area of speech was left "without appropriate standards to guide his action."

The upshot of these three lines of development is that today the speaker has a paramount claim to the use of the public forum which the state can subject to minimal traffic controls and to breach of peace limitations, but which the state cannot regulate in terms of the content of the message.

The fourth point goes to a special problem in connection with breaches of the peace, a problem not yet fully resolved by the courts and one which has special relevance to the Negro cases. A speaker may threaten a breach of peace in two ways, either by inciting to violence or by irritating an audience so that it responds with violence. In the second case, in which the audience is hostile, a difficult issue is posed. Apart from the "fighting words" point of the Chaplinsky[232] case, are there other circumstances in which the police, in order to keep tranquility, are entitled to arrest the speaker rather than the audience? The problem is a genuine puzzle either way it is decided. If the police can silence the speaker, the law in effect acknowledges a veto power in hecklers who can, by being hostile enough, get the law to silence any speaker of whom they do not approve. But the opposing view, that the police must go down with the speaker, has its obvious difficulties, too. And, until the advent of the Negro issues, the Court had thrown little light on where it would strike the balance. There is a dictum in the Hague case that uncontrolled official suppression of the speaker "cannot be made a substitute for the duty to maintain order."[233] In *Feiner,* Justice Black, in dissent, thought the police should have arrested the hecklers. And, finally, in his long, careful opinion in *Niemotko,* reviewing all the cases in the public forum area, Justice Frankfurter says clearly:

It is not a constitutional principle that, in acting
to preserve order, the police must proceed against
the crowd whatever its size and temper and not
against the speaker.[234]

As long as the Negroes stay on the streets and
the parks, their protests would appear to enjoy very
considerable protection in terms of the above points.
They, too, can commandeer the public forum. And
we would not be making any new law in protecting
them. There are, however, at least two somewhat
new points; first, the Negroes have shown some
tendency to use, for protest purposes, public property other than streets and parks. Is other public
property equally subject to a free-speech easement?
Secondly, what about the heckler veto problem in
connection with the Negro in the South? The Court
was near the issue in *Garner,* it will be recalled, but
none of the various opinions found it necessary to
confront directly whether the hostility generated by
the response of a Southern crowd to an otherwise
lawful Negro demonstration would make it possible
to stop the demonstration on the ground that it
threatened a breach of peace. Will the Constitution
require that in the South the police go down with
the Negro speakers? Or will the Court permit the
South one gigantic heckler veto?

Edwards v. *South Carolina,*[235] decided by the
Court on February 25, 1963, touches both of these
points. Once again, the issue is the constitutionality

of a conviction for breach of peace. This time, however, there are 187 Negro demonstrators involved, high-school and college students, and the location is state house grounds. The detailed facts are described by Justice Stewart for the majority of the Court, which upsets the convictions, in a passage well worth extended quotation:

> Late in the morning of March 2, 1961, the petitioners, high school and college students of the Negro race, met at the Zion Baptist Church in Columbia. From there, at about noon, they walked in separate groups of about 15 to the South Carolina State House grounds, an area of two city blocks open to the general public. Their purpose was "to submit a protest to the citizens of South Carolina, along with the Legislative Bodies of South Carolina, our feelings and our dissatisfaction with the present condition of discriminatory actions against Negroes in general and to let them know we were dissatisfied and that we would like for the laws which prohibited Negro privileges in this State to be removed."
> Already on the State House grounds when petitioners arrived, were some 30 or more law enforcement officers who had advance knowledge that petitioners were coming. Each group of petitioners entered the grounds through a driveway and parking area known in the record as the "horseshoe." As they entered, they were told by the law enforcement officials that they had a right as a citizen to go through State House grounds as any other citizen has, as long as they were peaceful. During the next half hour or 45 minutes, the petitioners in the same small groups walked single file or two abreast in an orderly way through

the grounds, each group carrying placards bearing
such messages as "I am proud to be a Negro" and
"Down with segregation."[236]

A crowd of several hundred onlookers gathered
on the adjacent sidewalks; they were, however, primarily curious rather than hostile, and there was
no interference with traffic. The police, it seems,
became apprehensive and advised the petitioners that
they would be arrested if they did not disperse in
fifteen minutes. The petitioners did not disperse,
but instead, engaged in what the Southern officials
describe as "boisterous, loud, and flamboyant" conduct. And after fifteen minutes, they were arrested
and "marched off to jail." The "flamboyant" conduct appears in the Court's recital of the facts, in
large part, to have been the sturdy singing of the
"Star Spangled Banner."

We would underscore several features in this
description of the facts. The connections between
Negro self-help and speech are here explicit since
placards are used; yet it is clear that had the
Negroes marched silently they would still have been
speaking the language of protest. Again one cannot,
I think, but be impressed with the grace and tact of
the performance; this is not a South American student riot hurling rocks at state house windows; this
is orderly protest to the public and to the state legislature. They have selected a public place where, as
citizens, they have a right to enter; they have picked
a time when the legislature is in session; they make

no threatening gestures, and are co-operative about not blocking traffic; they have the ironic wit to sing the "Star Spangled Banner" after the ultimatum of the police. And above all, they are young, and their statement of purpose is touching in its confidence in the democratic processes, including the one they were using—"to let them know we were dissatisfied and that we would like for the laws which prohibited Negro privileges in this State to be removed." Finally, there is an interesting tie back here to our concern in the first lecture with *Beauharnais* v. *Illinois,* in which, it will be recalled, the speech was also in the form of a petition for redress of grievances, but in which, except for Justice Black, the Court refused to take this aspect seriously.

The South Carolina courts having said that, under their law, breach of peace was a concept incapable of precise definition, the Court this time elects to accept the state court view that there was evidence in this record of violation of state law as defined by the state courts. They are abandoning, therefore, the strategy they had adopted in *Garner* of finding the record so barren of actual or potential violence as to make a conviction for breach of peace a violation of procedural due process. And they proceed in effect along the free-speech lines of Justice Harlan in *Garner.*

The reasoning is clear. First Amendment freedoms, we are reminded, are protected by the Fourteenth Amendment from invasion by the states.

"The circumstances in this case reflect an exercise of these basic constitutional rights in their most pristine and classic form."[237] In such cases, whatever the state law definitions, the Court can make an independent review of the "whole record." And an examination of the record reveals that they were convicted upon "evidence which showed no more than that the opinions which they were peaceably expressing were sufficiently opposed to the views of the majority of the community to attract a crowd and necessitate police protection."[238] *Feiner* v. *New York* is thus readily distinguished on its facts.

It should be noted that the Court comes close to the issue of Southern heckling. Since, however, the crowd itself appears to have been, in fact, peaceful, we cannot be sure from the Edwards case what the Court would say if, under comparable circumstances, the crowd had become overtly threatening. One final word. Justice Clark, as the lone dissenter, argues that *Feiner* is controlling since here there is a large crowd and some two hundred demonstrators and, recognizing the deep issue imbedded in the facts in *Edwards,* he sharply reminds the Court of Justice Frankfurter's dictum from *Niemotko* that there is no constitutional principle that says that whatever the situation the police must proceed against the crowd and not against the speaker.

The Edwards case thus captures in vivid form the image of Negro self-help as the exercise of First Amendment rights; indeed, Justice Stewart tells us it is the exercise of those rights "in their most pristine and classic form." And as long as the ceremony is orderly and tranquil, the demonstrators, whatever their message, can commandeer the streets, or the parks, or the state house grounds as their forum. We move next to the tantalizing possibility suggested by Justice Harlan's opinion in *Garner.* It will be remembered that he saw the sit-ins at the lunch counters as also engaging in free-speech activity as long as the owner had not withdrawn his consent. Our precise inquiry then is: does this activity lose its protected status entirely whenever we can say the property is private and the consent of the owner has been withdrawn? Does, that is, the doctrine of trespass always take precedence over the freedom of speech?

A distinction will prove helpful in pursuing so elusive and odd a point. We need to distinguish loosely between two categories of private property to which the doctrine of trespass would today apply. There is at one extreme the private home; that is, property in no sense open to the public and which is properly viewed as an asylum for privacy. We are not suggesting that the First Amendment empowers anyone to invade the home for the purpose of edifying, with a speech, its owners against their will. There is, however, the other extreme—where the property, although privately owned, is in an important sense open to the public; here values of

privacy are at a minimum.[239] The issue then nar-
rows to whether for this second category of private
property the owner retains absolute dominion over
the forum. We should, perhaps, make explicit how
subtle is the doctrinal game being played. Justice
Douglas argued in *Garner* that such property was
sufficiently in the public domain so that the owner
under the Fourteenth Amendment had lost his
power to discriminate among invitees on the basis
of race. We are exploring the alternative of saying
that such property is sufficiently public so that the
owner loses his power to deny the use of it as a
forum to one wishing to make a peaceful non-
obstructive speech.

One might say that these come down to the same
thing; and that if we are too fastidious for the
Douglas expansion of state action under the Fourteenth Amendment, it is very odd that we should
find congenial this expansion of the concept of the
public forum. But the two approaches do not seem
to me to come to quite the same thing; the first, I
would argue, requires a far larger revision of existing constitutional law doctrine than does the second.
In any event, the second puts the more novel and
flavorsome question.

There are perhaps, at best, a half dozen cases
that have some bearing on our point. *Martin* v.
Struthers,[240] decided in 1943, involved a city ordinance prohibiting door to door distribution of

handbills, circulars, or other advertisements. The defendant, a Jehovah Witness, distributed a leaflet announcing a religious meeting, and was convicted and fined ten dollars. There was some showing that the town was industrial, with men who worked night shifts, and that the ordinance had as one function the protection of their daytime sleep. Analytically, the case does not directly put the trespass issue; it was not known whether in any given instance the property owner had withdrawn the customary consent to having someone enter his property without invitation and ring his bell. The ordinance had simply substituted a single judgment of the community for the particular judgments of the individual owners. The case does involve, however, the problem of someone going onto private property to deliver a communication and the conditions under which he can constitutionally be prevented from so doing.

In a five to four decision, the Court, speaking through Justice Black, found the ordinance invalid. There is a strong paragraph on amateur methods of mass communication ending with the sentence: "Door to door distribution of circulars is essential to the poorly financed causes of little people." [241] The law, whatever its purposes in protecting privacy, freedom from annoyance, or prevention of crime must, holds Justice Black, protect the important First Amendment privilege of entering another's property in order to find out if he wishes to hear your message. The law must in this area leave to the householder "the full right to decide whether he will receive strangers as visitors." Further, the competing interest here can easily be accommodated by "making it an offense . . . to ring the bell of a householder who has appropriately indicated that he is unwilling to be disturbed." The vice of the ordinance is that it makes a person "a criminal trespasser if he enters the property of another for an innocent purpose without an explicit command from the owner to stay away." [242]

There is an interesting dissent by Justice Reed who sees dangers in the step the majority has taken. "The First Amendment," he observes, "does not compel a pedestrian to pause on the street to listen to the argument supporting another's views of religion or politics. Once the door is opened the visitor may not insert a foot and insist on a hearing. He certainly may not enter the home. To knock or ring, however, comes close to such invasions. . . . The ordinance seems a fair adjustment of the privileges of distributors and the rights of householders." [243]

Justice Black is clear that the doctrines of trespass may be used to punish those who "call at a home in defiance of the previously expressed will of the occupant." And Justice Reed in dissent is even clearer that the doctrine of trespass sets the limits of free speech on private property. Closely read, however, the majority opinion makes it evident that the real concern is with the captive audience; the distributor cannot by doctrines of property be cut off from the willing audience.

Marsh v. *Alabama*[244] in 1946 comes somewhat closer to the precise problem of Negro protest on private property. The defendant, a Jehovah Witness, is convicted of criminal trespass for distributing religious literature on the sidewalks of a company-owned town in violation of a company rule, of which she had notice. The Court in a five to three decision, with Justice Reed again writing for the dissent, upsets the conviction. In legal theory the sidewalks in the company town are owned by the company and are private property; hence the majority decision does in this instance subordinate the owner's power to use the trespass sanction to the interest in free speech.

The case, however, is not so squarely in point because of the peculiar nature of a company town, a circumstance on which the Court relies heavily. As Justice Frankfurter says in his concurring opinion, "But a company owned town is a town."[245] The fact that title is in the company is regarded by the Court as a formality; this is still a political community and had it been organized along customary political lines, with the property all privately owned, "all those owners together could not have set up a municipal government with sufficient power to pass an ordinance completely barring the distribution of religious literature."[246] Wherever title may be, the functional needs of a community for the free flow of communications are decisive. "There is," says Justice Black, "no more reason for depriving these people of the liberties guaranteed by the First and Fourteenth Amendments than there is for curtailing these freedoms with respect to any other citizen."[247]

Justice Reed in dissent reads as though he had anticipated the present argument. He sees a broad principle behind the decision.

> What the present decision establishes as a principle is that one may remain on private property against the will of the owner and contrary to the law of the state so long as the only objection to his presence is that he is exercising an asserted right to spread there his religious views. . . . This is the first case to extend by law the privilege of religious exercises beyond public places or to private places without the assent of the owner. As the rule now announced permits this intrusion, without possibility of protection of property by law, and apparently is equally applicable to the freedom of speech and the press, it seems appropriate to express a dissent to this novel Constitutional doctrine.[248]

Martin v. *Struthers* is distinguishable, he argues, since in the instant case the trespass is found only after explicit warning by the owner. The Reed dissent concludes with another passage directly in point:

> Our Constitution guarantees to every man the right to express his views in an orderly fashion.

An essential element of "orderly" is that the man shall also have a right to use the place he chooses for his exposition. The rights of the owner which the Constitution protects as well as the right of free speech are not outweighed by the interests of the trespasser even though he trespasses in behalf of religion or free speech. We cannot say that Jehovah's Witnesses can claim the privilege of a license which has never been granted to hold their meetings in other private places merely because the owner has admitted the public to them for other limited purposes.[249]

It has been fashionable in recent years to construe *Marsh* as an exciting state action case on the view that it holds that a company town is a de facto town, subject to the normal inhibitions the Constitution imposes on government.[250] On this interpretation it does not aid the present argument, since the property we are concerned with in the Negro protest cases is by no means so public as a company town. If, however, we read the majority opinion as Justice Reed has read it in his dissent, *Marsh* is precisely in point and supports the thesis that the public interest in speech may override the private owner's autonomy. Further, Justice Black sees the company owner as exercising a third-party veto cutting the citizens of the town off from this flow of communication, a point which has considerable relevance for speech by sit-in.

In 1948, in *Watchtower Bible and Tract Society v. Metropolitan Life Insurance Co.*,[251] the New York

Court of Appeals decided a case which combined in effect the facts of *Martin* v. *Struthers* and *Marsh* v. *Alabama* and indicated a conservative reading of both precedents. Once again we have Jehovah Witnesses seeking to distribute their literature; but this time the forum is a gigantic housing development consisting of some 171 interrelated apartment houses, accommodating some 35,000 people. All apartments are rented under written leases from the defendant owner. A regulation of the owner prohibits entry into the buildings for the purpose of soliciting or distributing, except upon prior written consent from a tenant. The use of the streets and sidewalks within this residential community is left open; it is the use of the hallways that is prohibited. The Witnesses sue to enjoin enforcement of the regulation. The New York court unanimously upholds it.

The Court limits *Marsh* to a holding that the sidewalk in the company town was "in appearance and use an ordinary public sidewalk." It recognizes the doctrine of a right to the public forum and quotes the basic statement of Justice Roberts from the Hague case. The Court then adds wryly: "A narrow inner hallway on an upper floor of an apartment house is hardly an appropriate place at which to demand the free exercise of those ancient rights."[252] Like Justice Reed in *Marsh* and *Struthers,* Judge Desmond for the New York court would let the boundaries of private property set the limits of the First Amendment. "No case we know of extends the reach of the Bill of Rights so far as to proscribe the reasonable regulation by an owner of conduct inside his multiple dwelling."[253]

In two other contexts the Court has had occasion in recent years to approach the problem we are concerned with. The two sound truck cases, *Saia*[254] and *Kovacs*,[255] in 1947 and 1949, put to the court the problem of a speaker hurling his message across property lines. In *Saia* an ordinance limiting the use of sound trucks was, it will be recalled, held unconstitutional; while, two years later, in *Kovacs* a somewhat different ordinance limiting their use was upheld. It might be thought that the two cases would be helpful for our present concerns and would enable us to explore whether, if the message may come in across private property boundaries, the speaker can enter with it. The Court's handling, however, is disappointing, and has left unclear precisely what is the status of the sound truck itself. *Saia* appears to have gone off on the fact that the ordinance, there invalidated, required a permit with apparently unfettered discretion in the public official to grant or deny it. It, therefore, fell on familiar prior restraint principles. In *Kovacs* the ban of the ordinance was absolute, but the majority in upholding the ordinance read it as limited to the emitting of "loud and raucous" noises, the dissenters read it as banning all sound trucks. In general the Court saw the problem as similar to that in *Cox* v. *New*

Hampshire, that is, the enforcing of a non-content regulation in the fashion of *Roberts' Rules of Order.* "The right to speak one's mind would often be an empty privilege in a place and at a time beyond the protecting hand of the guardian of public order."[256] On this view the Kovacs case holds no more than that the state, in the interests of speech and privacy, may bar loud noises which interfere with other speech and are, in the parliamentary sense, out of order.

The majority opinion, however, is by Justice Reed who will be remembered from his dissents in *Struthers* and *Marsh.* There are once again in his opinion some strong suggestions of the trespass and captive audience themes. "This Court," he advises, "never intimated that the visitor could insert a foot in the door and insist on a hearing. . . . We do not think the *Struthers* case requires us to expand this interdiction of legislation to include ordinances against obtaining an audience for the broadcaster's ideas by way of sound trucks with loud and raucous noises on city streets." He then adds two sentences that make the sound truck problem more in point. "The unwilling listener is not like the passer-by who may be offered a pamphlet in the street but cannot be made to take it. In his home or on the street he is practically helpless to escape this interference with his privacy by loud speakers except through the protection of the municipality." The image of the captive audience threat in the sound

truck device is also vivid in the next few sentences:
the city dweller cannot be left "at the mercy of
advocates of particular religious, social, or political
persuasions. . . . The right of free speech is guaranteed every citizen that he may reach the minds
of willing listeners. . . . "[257]

Justice Black in dissent, it should be noted, does
not disagree that the speaker is not to be privileged
to capture his audience. His dissent rather goes to
what he sees as the unnecessary breadth of the
ordinance and to the need of protecting unorthodox
media of communication so as to avoid favoring the
owners of more customary mass media.

Thus far trespassing and capturing the audience
have appeared as twin issues in the cases. In *Public
Utilities Commission* v. *Pollak*,[258] decided in 1952,
the captive audience issue, standing alone, comes to
the Court. The problem arises over the playing of
background music on the public busses and street
cars in Washington, D.C. The busses and street
cars are operated by the Capital Transit Company
as a public utility under the authority of Congress
and subject to supervisory control by the Public
Utilities Commission of the District. The commission had held hearings on the transit broadcasting,
which had become something of a *cause cèlébre* in
Washington at the time,[259] and had then dismissed
its investigation. The Court of Appeals for the
District, speaking through Judge Edgerton, had
found the arrangement so intimately involving the

federal government as to constitute state action and
had found the state action a violation of the First
and Fifth Amendments in that it captured an audience and interfered with privacy. The Supreme
Court reversed. It recognized that there was sufficient state action here to raise constitutional issues;
but since nothing but music and brief advertising
was broadcast and since it was not shown to interfere with conversation, it found no constitutional
violations. The matter was simply one for the
discretion of the commission.

Justices Black and Douglas were, however, sharply
sensitive to the possibilities that inhere in audience
capture. Justice Black concurred, insofar as the
ruling was limited to the broadcasting of music. But
he added the warning: "Subjecting Capital Transit's passengers to the broadcasting of news, public
speeches, views or propaganda . . . would violate
the First Amendment."[260]

Justice Douglas dissented. There was too much
of Orwell's *1984* in the transit broadcast arrangement. His opinion is an eloquent statement of the
importance of privacy to freedom of belief and
speech; and as in the Gibson case, we see once
again a surprisingly intimate connection between the
Fourth Amendment and the First. "The present
case involves a form of coercion to make people
listen." Although the circumstances of the present
case are benign and the grievance, as such, is trivial,
the point is so important that government must be

denied at the threshold any claim whatsoever to compel men to listen to its messages. "The right to be let alone is indeed the beginning of all freedom. . . . Freedom of religion and freedom of speech guaranteed by the First Amendment give more than the privilege to worship, to write, to speak as one chooses; they give freedom not to do nor to act as the government chooses." Justice Douglas therefore concludes: "If liberty is to flourish, government should never be allowed to force people to listen to any radio program."[261]

Finally, in describing the plight of the poor passenger who does not choose to hear, he observes: "One who tunes in an offensive program at home can turn it off or tune in another station, as he wishes. One who hears disquieting or unpleasant programs in public places, *such as restaurants,* can get up and leave. But the man on the streetcar has no choice but to sit and listen, or perhaps to sit and try not to listen."[262] Rarely in the history of the Court has a trivial amusing fact situation given rise to such wide ranging and intense philosophizing by the members of the Court.

Once again pursuit of the special problems raised by the Negro protest movement has opened to a broad vista of free-speech theory. The only value which the Court may hold to counterbalance fully the right to speak appears to be the right not to listen. However frightening the Orwellian *1984* imagery and however eloquent the Douglas identification of freedom and privacy, the issue is not without its perplexities. The freedom not to listen would appear to include the freedom to avoid exposure to alien ideas, thus making the closed mind a principal feature of the open society. Further, on reflection, it would appear that the entire compulsory education system on which democracy so much rests is a utilization of the captive audience device. But these, important as they are, are concerns for another day.

How does our sit-in problem look after this review of the authorities which bear, at least remotely, on it? Quite clearly it poses a novel issue which prior law cannot be said to have put to rest. Further, one can, I think, say with some confidence that it is the captive audience evil and not the trespass that is seriously troublesome. *Marsh* is authority that at least under some circumstances the automatic veto power of the private owner must yield to the counter values of speech and the claim to a forum. *Cox* is a reminder that a variety of non-content controls designed to keep things orderly can be applied to normal speech and hence to the oblique symbolic speech of the sit-in. Does the thesis then collapse in face of the captive audience problem? Must the Southerners who do not wish to hear the silent protest of the Negro sit-ins have it forced upon them by privileging the trespass? I am not at all confident of the answer. There are some aspects of the captive audience here, but basically it seems to me the relevant audience is free to leave, and the owner, in invoking trespass, is seeking to cut them off from a message they may be willing to hear. Having so carefully raised and nurtured the issue and brought it to this point, I am happy to leave it unresolved. I have just three final thoughts on it. First, insofar as the audience exercises its option to walk away from the silent Negro speech, it may also be walking away from the owner's business establishment; and the Negro speech may thus have economic repercussions of the kind which made it so difficult to treat picketing as pure free speech. Secondly, when all the pieces of the argument are put together, it is evident that it would exact apparently a narrow concession; only the tranquil quiet demonstration would qualify. We would paradoxically be extending the protection of the First Amendment largely to silent speech. I suspect, however, that this may be no small matter. The genius of the Negro protest has resided in its rhetoric of patient silence. Indeed, it could well be said that the movement has been guided by a sure instinct for silent speech. Finally, there is the large question of whether the Southern audience can be forced, at least briefly, to hear the message of Negro grievances or whether, even for such high purposes, we cannot permit an audience to be captured. In the end, it may be a terrible irony of the Negro protest movement that it is speech only to the Northern audiences.

IV

Sequel to "Trespass and the First Amendment"

O N JUNE 22, 1964, the last day of the term, the
Supreme Court took a long-awaited step and
disposed of the many sit-in cases that had been
pending. Since the third lecture is centrally concerned with the sit-in problem and outlines a possible
First Amendment approach to it, there is point
in adding a brief postscript to bring the rapidly
unfolding legal story up-to-date.

Of the some fourteen sit-in cases in all, nine were
disposed of summarily,[263] and five received opinions,
Robinson, Barr, Griffin, Bouie, and *Bell.*[264] For
present purposes there are three important points
to note about this new batch of cases. First, once
again the Court avoids reaching the central constitutional issue, perhaps in the hope that the newly
enacted federal legislation may render the question
moot.[265] Secondly, except for a brief passage in the
dissenting opinion in the Bell case, the opinions are
totally silent on the First Amendment approach here
raised. Thirdly, and perhaps of the most general

legal interest, there is a new alignment of judges
with Justices Harlan, White, and Black joining in
dissent in three cases, and with Mr. Justice Black,
in the Bell case, writing a profoundly interesting
and moving opinion, affirming the conviction of the
sit-ins.

It will be recalled that the sit-in problem had
been before the Court on two other occasions,
resulting in the 1961 decision in *Garner*[266] and
the 1963 decisions in *Shuttlesworth,*[267] *Peterson,*[268]
and *Lombard.*[269] Arguably the sit-in might be proceeded against under a breach of peace statute or
under a criminal trespass statute. In *Garner* the
Court had outlawed the breach of peace approach,
and in the 1963 series the Court had found specific
flaws in the trespass cases presented to it but
had carefully left undecided the fate of a "pure"
trespass case.

The current cases continue the game, with the
South still failing to get a "pure" trespass case to
the Court. In *Barr* v. *City of Columbia,*[270] the Court
upset convictions for a breach of peace; it followed
the Warren opinion in *Garner* and held that there
was simply no evidence of the crime. It is worth
noting that the opinion was by Justice Black, who
dissents in three of the other sit-in cases, and that
the decision is, as it was in *Garner,* unanimous.[271]

A second case, *Robinson* v. *Florida,*[272] although
involving trespass,[273] is readily disposed on the

grounds that the restaurant facilities are segregated pursuant to a regulation of the board of health,[274] thus disclosing the kind of state action that had proved fatal to the convictions in *Peterson.* Once again, the decision is unanimous, and once again the opinion is by Justice Black.

In the remaining three cases, the device used to avoid the constitutional issue is less persuasive to the Justices, and there are strong dissents. In *Griffin* v. *Maryland,*[275] the majority once again finds too many traces of state action, and the convictions are upset. This time it is an amusement park which is privately owned and the owner's policy of segregation is enforced by a private police officer who has been deputized. The arrangements with the deputy sheriff are undoubtedly more intimate than the customary relationship of a private property owner and the police, but it is difficult to see why this difference should matter;[276] and this is precisely what the three dissenters, Justices Harlan, White, and Black, say in a brief opinion by Justice Harlan:[277] "It seems clear to me, however, that the involvement of the state is no different from what it would have been had the arrests been made by a regular policeman dispatched from police headquarters."

Bouie v. *City of Columbia*[278] is handled in a more complex way. The South Carolina trespass statute speaks in terms of "entry . . . after notice from

the owner prohibiting such entry." The sit-in is at
the lunch counter of a drug store which in other
departments caters to Negro customers. There is
at the time the defendants enter and sit down no
explicit notice prohibiting their entry. However,
when they are asked to leave, the defendants refuse
and are arrested.

The South Carolina court, apparently to meet
defendants' challenge that *Garner* controls because
there is no evidence that they violated the statute,
construes the statute to cover also the act of remaining on the premises after a request to leave. Since
the state court is, of course, the final arbiter of the
meaning of its own statute, the Supreme Court is
foreclosed this time from using the *Garner* technique. The majority,[279] in an opinion by Justice
Brennan, still manages to avoid the underlying
constitutional issue of equal protection by finding
a procedural due process flaw in the case. Essentially the argument is that the state statute carried
no warning at the time of the sit-in that it covered
what the state court was later to decide that it did.
It is, therefore, an instance of ex post facto legislation, no less subject to constitutional infirmity
because it is an act of the judiciary than if it were
an act of the legislature. The vice is the "unfore-
seeable and retroactive judicial expansion of narrow
and precise statutory language." The rationale of
the majority is somewhat buttressed by the fact that

the South Carolina legislature amended the statute,
shortly after the sit-ins occurred, to cover explicitly
those who enter with consent but refuse to leave
when the consent is withdrawn.

This logic invites a fuller examination than we
can spare for it under the present circumstances.
It gives the Court a possible new weapon to use
against Southern state courts which may be tempted,
under the exacerbations of the Negro protest, to
arbitrary, albeit definitive, constructions of their
own statutes. It also raises a first-rate jurispru-
dential puzzle: If the state court is the definitive
reader of the statute and if it finds the "new"
meaning in the statute, must not the Supreme Court
accept, not only that the meaning is there now, but
also that the meaning was somehow always there
and hence gave notice to the citizens of the state?
And to make a less formalistic point, did not custom
tell the defendants that they were not invited to
lunch? Finally, does the constitutional need for a
fair warning depend on the actual expectations of
these defendants—who intended to be arrested—or
an objective reading of the statute?

In any event, Justices Black, Harlan, and White
will not go along, and it is Justice Black who writes
the dissent, relying largely on what he says to the
comparable point in his dissenting opinion in *Bell
v. Maryland.*[280] The dissenters take a less critical
view of the state precedents offered in support of

the "new" construction; given the old common-law concept of trespass *ab initio*,[281] it is fair to say that trespass under the state law had always covered the case of refusal to leave. What moves the dissenters, however, are not the niceties of the law of trespass but that the very point of the sit-in was to protest against the segregated restaurant policy. It seems artificial to say that they were "misled" into thinking they were engaging in lawful conduct.[282] The point was, therefore, not substantial enough to check the momentum of the dissenters toward reaching and resolving the basic constitutional issue—which is the story of the last of the cases, *Bell* v. *Maryland*.

Bell represents a major effort by the Court, the various opinions totaling some one hundred and twenty pages. The facts and the state trespass statute are by now familiar. This time it is a restaurant proper, and there is no ambiguity engendered in the fact that Negroes are welcome as customers in other parts of the premises.

Again Justice Brennan writes for the majority. Perhaps because the "fair warning" tactic will not work as well with a restaurant proper, he decides not to rely on *Bouie* but to find yet another way to avoid the underlying constitutional issue. He finds it in the circumstance that after the convictions had been affirmed by the Maryland Court of Appeals but while the case was pending in the United States Supreme Court, the Maryland legislature had enacted a public accommodations law making it unlawful to deny entry upon the basis of "race, creed, color, or national origin." The law, said Justice Brennan, thus "abolished the crime" for which the defendants had been convicted. He would, therefore, remand the case to the Maryland courts to see what response they would have to this dramatic change in state policy. In support of this move, he cites ample Maryland authority to the effect that the repeal of a criminal law in the absence of a saving clause will cause the dismissal of pending cases. He recognizes that in the instant case the law has not directly been repealed and the cases cannot easily be said to be pending under state law since the convictions had already been affirmed by the highest state court. He is not sure what, if anything, the Maryland courts will do with the matter on remand, but he deems it appropriate to remand "so that the state court may consider the effects of the supervening charges in state law." His key point is that the change in state law is far more dramatic than a mere repeal and that, therefore, the general savings clause is not applicable. What had previously been a criminal act on the part of the defendant, he is now entitled to do as an affirmative right. There is, therefore, sufficient basis for the expectation that the matter would be of interest to the state supreme court to warrant returning the case to it.

Justice Brennan enlists only two wholehearted allies, Justices Clark and Stewart. The six remaining Justices all agree that the constitutional issue should be reached[283] and proceed to discuss it at length. They split evenly as to how they would decide it, thus preventing the Court from officially passing on it. However, it is this exchange of views between the two wings of the Court on the constitutional issues that makes the Bell case a memorable precedent on the basic issue of the scope of federal power under the Fourteenth Amendment.

It is at this point that we have Justice Black and Justice Harlan[284] joining forces with Justice White in dissent. In a way, it is curious that they are so insistent on confronting and putting to rest the underlying issue. It has been a strong practice of the Court not to decide constitutional issues unless absolutely necessary; indeed, this judicial "economy" had been one of Mr. Justice Frankfurter's first principles.[285] Furthermore, there is the obvious practical circumstance that the pending civil rights legislation might keep the sit-in question from ever coming back to the Court. The dissenters are moved, however, by a counter "practical" consideration. Since they so firmly hold there is no constitutional infirmity in the sit-in convictions for trespass, they appear to think it unfair, uncandid, and imprudent to lull the public and the protest movement into a false sense of constitutional security.[286] Thus, after noting that the rule about not unnecessarily reaching constitutional questions is simply a matter of court practice and not "an inexorable command,"[287] Justice Black concludes:

> We should feel constrained to decide this question even if we thought the state law invalid. In this case, however, we believe that the state law is a valid exercise of state legislative power, that the question is properly before us, and that the national interest imperatively calls for an authoritative decision of the question by this court.

The other trio of Justices who concur in the decision but would reach the constitutional issue and decide it favorably to the petitioners consists of the Chief Justice, Justices Douglas and Goldberg. There are separate opinions by Justice Douglas and Justice Goldberg, elaborately stating their views on the constitutional point. It is well beyond the scope of the present essay to examine and evaluate the Black, Douglas, and Goldberg essays on the reach of the Fourteenth Amendment, although these are the most durably important features of the case. Justice Black offers an interesting and helpful interpretation of that mysterious precedent outlawing restrictive covenants, *Shelley* v. *Kraemer*;[288] Justice Douglas, varying the rationales he had previously urged in *Garner*[289] and *Lombard*,[290] makes a novel argument keyed to the corporate nature of the private property owners in the sit-in cases, and

Justice Goldberg makes a bold bid to put his broad interpretation of the Fourteenth Amendment on historical grounds.

For our more limited purposes, there are three characteristics of the debate to note. First, the Black-Harlan-White position is narrower and more subtle than first appears. They are careful to say only that Section 1 of the Fourteenth Amendment, standing alone, does not make the sit-in convictions invalid. They leave open whether the reach of *federal* power under congressional legislation pursuant to Section 5[291] might not protect the sit-in. They do not, therefore, pass either on the status of the troubled precedent of the Civil Rights Cases of 1883,[292] since it dealt with federal legislation, or on the status of the then pending civil rights legislation of 1964. The care with which they save the case of congressional legislation suggests that they will find the public accommodation provisions of the Civil Rights Act of 1964 constitutional, even apart from the commerce clause. Given this subtlety, it is perhaps somewhat more puzzling, then, that they felt so compelled, in "the national interest," to make public their constitutional "truth."

The final points may conveniently be noted together. They involve the role of Justice Black and the response of the Court to a First Amendment approach to the sit-ins—thus at long last bringing this comment back to the principal theme of the third lecture. Near the end of his long opinion, Justice Black touches the argument that the sit-in can be viewed as a form of free speech. Although he has been second to none in the history of the Court in his steadfast and eloquent support of freedom of speech, Justice Black can see nothing to the point in this context; and Justice Harlan, the father of the thought in *Garner,* joins silently in the opinion. "It is wholly clear," Justice Black tells us, "that the Maryland statute here is directed not against what the petitioners said but against what they did. . . . " The whole free-speech analogy is characterized brusquely as "a bootstrap argument," and he adds: "The right to freedom of expression is a right to express views—not a right to force other people to supply a platform or a pulpit."

The distinction between the public and the private forum is thus vigorously maintained; the prior question always is: Does the speaker have right to be where he is? To answer, on Justice Black's view, the question we had put in the third lecture[293]—the doctrine of trespass does always takes precedence over the freedom of speech.

None of the other Justices advert to the free-speech possibility in any of the sit-in cases; and with the federal legislation now available, it appears likely that this engaging speech issue will never be passed upon by the Court. Justice Black may, there-fore, have spoken the last word on the point. In any event, the last words of his dissent in *Bell* v. *Maryland* are superb:

> A great purpose of freedom of speech and press is to provide a forum for settlement of acrimonious disputes peaceably, without resort to intimidation, force, or violence. The experience of ages points to the inexorable fact that people are frequently stirred to violence when property which the law recognizes as theirs is forcibly invaded or occupied by others. Trespass laws are born of this experience. They have been, and doubtless still are, important features of any government dedicated, as this country is, to a rule of law. Whatever power it may allow the States or grant to the Congress to regulate the use of private property, the Constitution does not confer upon any group the right to substitute rule by force for rule by law. Force leads to violence, violence to mob conflicts, and these to rule by the strongest groups with control of the most deadly weapons. Our Constitution, noble work of wise men, was designed—all of it—to chart a quite different course: to "establish Justice, and insure domestic Tranquility * * * and secure the Blessings of Liberty to ourselves and our Posterity." At times the rule of law seems too slow to some for the settlement of their grievances. But it is the plan our Nation has chosen to preserve both "Liberty" and equality for all. On that plan we have put our trust and staked our future. This constitutional rule of law has served us well. Maryland's trespass law does not depart from it. Nor shall we.

Notes

Introduction

1. 321 U.S. 649 (1944).

2. 334 U.S. 1 (1948).

3. 347 U.S. 483 (1954).

4. Wechsler, *Toward Neutral Principles of Constitutional Law,* 73 HARV.L.REV. 1 (1959).

5. BOGGS, THE AMERICAN REVOLUTION: PAGES FROM A NEGRO WORKER'S NOTEBOOK (1963).

6. See, for example, Smith, *Sequel to Workmen's Compensation Acts,* 27 HARV.L.REV. 235, 344 (1913); Blum & Kalven, *Public Law Perspectives on a Private Law Problem —Auto Compensation Plans,* 31 U.CHI.L.REV. 641, 662–65 (1964).

7. GREGORY & KALVEN, CASES AND MATERIALS ON TORTS 992–94 (1959).

8. Republished in 1948, with other essays, under the title, POLITICAL FREEDOM: THE CONSTITUTIONAL POWERS OF THE PEOPLE.

9. Emerson, *Toward a General Theory of the First Amendment,* 72 YALE L.J. 877 (1963).

10. 343 U.S. 250 (1952).

11. 376 U.S. 254 (1964). As noted in the Preface, I have elected, as the lesser evil, to leave the "timing" of the lectures as it was when they were given in April, 1964. At that time, the *New York Times* case was just one month old. Since the date of the lectures, I have had opportunity to review the *Times* case in considerable detail; see Kalven, *The New York Times Case: A Note on the Central Meaning of the First Amendment,* [1964] Sup.Ct. Rev. 191.

12. 372 U.S. 549 (1963).

13. 368 U.S. 157 (1961).

14. A few months later, the Court did just that. For a brief discussion of these 1964 sit-in cases, see "Sequel to 'Trespass and the First Amendment,' " pp. 161 *infra*.

I

15. *Supra,* note 10.

16. The new code merged the three prior criminal-libel laws into a single brief statute keyed to breach of peace. Smith-Hurd, ILL.STAT.ANN. (1961), chap. 38, §§ 27-1, 27-2, and the committee comments.

17. *Supra,* note 11.

18. See generally, Riesman, *Democracy and Defamation: Control of Group Libel,* 42 COLUM.L.REV. 727 (1942) ; Tannehaus, *Group Libel,* 35 CORNELL L.Q. 261 (1950) ; Note, 47 COLUM.L.REV. 595 (1947) ; CHAFEE, GOVERNMENT AND MASS COMMUNICATIONS 116 *et seq.* (1947) ; Beth, *Group Libel and Free Speech,* 39 MINN.L.REV. 167 (1955) ; Note, 61 YALE L.J. 252 (1955).

19. Riesman, *op. cit.,* note 18, at 730.

20. Compare Kalven, *The Metaphysics of the Law of Obscenity,* [1960] Sup.Ct.Rev. 1.

21. Note, 22 IND.L.J. 295 (1947) ; IND.STAT.ANN. §10–960 (1962) (the section title is "Racketeering in Hatred").

22. 340 U.S. 290, 299 (1951).

23. Cf. PEKELIS, LAW AND SOCIAL ACTION (1947) ; Note, 58 YALE L.J. 524, 589–94 (1949).

24. See generally, CHAFEE, FREE SPEECH IN THE UNITED STATES (1941) ; Meiklejohn, *op. cit., supra,* note 8; Emerson, *op. cit., supra,* note 9; Mendelson, *Clear and Present Danger—From Schenck to Dennis,* 52 COLUM.L.REV. 313 (1952).

25. *Op. cit., supra,* note 9, at 912.

26. Schenck v. United States, 249 U.S. 47 (1919).

27. Whitney v. California, 274 U.S. 357, 375 *et seq.* (1927).

28. See especially his concurring opinion in Dennis v. United States, 341 U.S. 494, 517 (1951).

29. Compare Kalven & Rosenfield, *The Contemporary Function of the Class Suit,* 8 U.Chi.L.Rev. 684, 707 n. 73 (1941).

30. *Supra,* note 8.

31. United States v. Dennis, 183 F.2d. 201 (2d Cir. 1950).

32. Justice Frankfurter speaks of these dissents as coming to the Court with "a special momentum of respect." And, in any event, it is striking, given Gitlow v. New York, 268 U.S. 652 (1925) as a precedent, how hard the Justices had to work to sustain the constitutionality of the Smith Act and to make peace with Holmes and Brandeis.

33. Biddle, *Symposium on Civil Liberties,* 9 Am.L.S. Rev. 889, 892 (1941).

34. *Op. cit.,* note 18, at 601–2.

35. See generally on seditious libel, Chafee, Free Speech in the United States, 19 *et seq.,* 497–516 (1941); 2 Stephen, History of the Criminal Law 299, 353 (1883); Levy, The Legacy of Suppression, 1–17 (1960).

36. See Kalven, *The Law of Defamation and the First Amendment* in University of Chicago Law School Conference on the Arts, Publishing and the Law 3 (1952).

37. Masses Pub. Co. v. Patten, 244 Fed. 535 (S.D.N.Y. 1917).

38. This thesis is argued more fully in Kalven, *op. cit., supra,* note 11.

39. 1 Stat. 596 (1798).

40. 250 U.S. 616, 630 (1919).

41. The Espionage Act of 1917, as amended in 1918, carried several sections which echoed closely the idiom of seditious libel; see Chafee, *op. cit., supra,* note 35, at 38–42. It was in response to this argument of counsel that Justice Holmes uttered his important dictum; see note 40, *supra.*

42. Corwin, *Freedom of Speech and Press Under the First Amendment,* 30 Yale L.J. 48 (1920).

43. Hall, *Free Speech in War Times,* 21 Colum.L.Rev. 526 (1921).

44. Vance, *Freedom of Speech and the Press*, 2 MINN. L.REV. 239 (1918).

45. CROSSKEY, POLITICS AND THE CONSTITUTION 767 (1953).

46. For a thoughtful critique of the Levy thesis, see Anastaplo, Book Review, 39 N.Y.U.L.REV. 735 (1964).

47. LEVY, JEFFERSON AND CIVIL LIBERTIES: THE DARKER SIDE (1963).

48. Terminiello v. Chicago, 337 U.S. 1 (1949).

49. *Id.*, at 13–14.

50. Kunz v. New York, 340 U.S. 290 (1951).

51. See text, *supra,* p. 21.

52. (1917) Ill. Laws 362.

53. See Klapprott v. New Jersey, 127 N.J.L. 395, 22 A.2d 877 (1941); Note, 47 COLUM.L.REV. 595 (1947).

54. 408 Ill. 512, 97 N.E.2d 343 (1951).

55. 36 F. Supp. 708 (D. C. Ill. 1941). The United States Supreme Court affirmed the refusal of the three-judge court to grant injunction relief, but did not pass on the constitutionality of the Illinois statute, (314 U.S. 573 1941).

56. 343 U.S. 250, 266 (1952).

57. 315 U.S. 568, 571–72 (1942).

58. 343 U.S. 250, 258 (1952).

59. *Ibid.*

60. *Supra,* note 28.

61. 283 U.S. 359 (1931).

62. Note, 109 U.PA.L.REV. 67 (1960).

63. 333 U.S. 507 (1948).

64. 343 U.S. 495 (1952).

65. 354 U.S. 476 (1957).

66. 340 U.S. 290, 284–85 (1951).

67. There are suggestions of the distinction in earlier opinions; see Holmes, dissenting in Gitlow v. New York, 268

U.S. 652 672 (1925) and Hand in Dennis v. United States, 183 F.2d. 201, 208 (2d Cir. 1950).

68. Palko v. Connecticut, 302 U.S. 319 (1937).

69. 341 U.S. 494, 561, 568 (1951).

70. A thoughtful theoretical argument for federalism in the free-speech area has recently been put forward. See Anastaplo, "Notes on the First Amendment" (Ph.D. thesis, University of Chicago, 1964).

71. See Kalven, *op. cit., supra,* note 20, at 21–23.

72. 367 U.S. 643 (1961).

73. 372 U.S. 335 (1963).

74. Once again see note 11. The two-tier thesis may have been finally put to rest in the *New York Times* case; see Kalven, *op. cit., supra,* note 11.

75. 343 U.S. 250, 284 (1952).

76. *Id.* at 284–85. (Italics added.)

77. *Id.* at 286.

78. *Ibid.*

79. *Ibid.*

80. *Id.* at 286–87.

81. *Id.* at 275.

82. See Kalven, *The Congressional Testing of Linus Pauling: The Legal Framework,* in GRODZINS & RABINOWITCH, THE ATOMIC AGE 466 (1963). In somewhat the same way, it is interesting that the Court handles the advertisement in the *Times* case as an "editorial" (see 376 U.S. 254, 266 [1964]) and readily handles the leaflet in Valentine v. Chrestensen, 316 U.S. 52 (1942) as "commercial."

83. 343 U.S. 250, 271–72 (1952).

84. *Id.* at 273.

85. *Id.* at 275.

86. *Id.* at 273.

87. Kalven, *op. cit., supra,* note 20. For a further analysis of the impact of the *Times* case on this two-level approach, see Kalven, *op. cit., supra,* note 11.

88. The *Times* case changes this with respect to seditious libel, but it is still true that the Court has not seriously inventoried other categories of speech in terms of the history; see Kalven, *op. cit., supra,* note 20, at 9.

89. 315 U.S. 568, 571–72 (1942).

90. CHAFEE, FREE SPEECH IN THE UNITED STATES 149 (1941).

91. LEVI, AN INTRODUCTION TO LEGAL REASONING (1949).

92. Cahn, *Justice Black and the First Amendment "Absolutes": A Public Interview,* 37 N.Y.U.L.REV. 549 (1962).

93. *Id.* at 557.

94. 376 U.S. 254 (1964).

95. See generally Noel, *Defamation of Public Officials,* 49 COLUM.L.REV. 875 (1949) ; Veeder, *Freedom of Public Discussion,* 23 HARV.L.REV. 413 (1910) ; Riesman, *Democracy and Defamation: Fair Game and Fair Comment,* 42 COLUM. L.REV. 1085, 1282 (1942).

96. 50 T.L.R. 581 (C.A. 1934).

97. For a more detailed assessment of whether the Alabama judgment was a sham, see Kalven, *op. cit., supra,* note 11 ; and on shams, see note 157, *infra.*

98. The one possible difference between the two dissenting opinions is that Justice Goldberg is explicit that he would retain libel actions for comment on the *private* life of a public official.

99. The radical quality of placing the choice between the majority and the minority rule on constitutional grounds is attested to by the close and careful balancing of the conflicting policies in the leading case for the minority view, Coleman v. McLennan, 78 Kan. 711, 98 Pac. 281 (1908).

100. 376 U.S. 254, 273 (1964).

101. *Id.* at 276.

102. The Court expressly acknowledges its debt to LEVY, THE LEGACY OF SUPPRESSION, chap. vi (1960). Professor Levy himself does not find his "revisionist" history of the First Amendment binding or distressing, because the Constitution, at least in the area of civil liberties, need not, on his

view, "be anchored in the past."—*Id.* at 4; see also note 46, *supra.*

103. As to whether it was inconsistent for the majority not to have gone the whole way to an absolute privilege, see Kalven, *op. cit., supra,* note 11.

104. 360 U.S. 564 (1959).

105. 376 U.S. 254, 282 (1964).

106. *Op. cit., supra,* note 8, at 34–36.

107. Kingsley Pictures Corp. v. Regents, 360 U.S. 684, 688–89 (1959).

108. 310 U.S. 296, 310 (1940).

109. Bridges v. California, 314 U.S. 252 (1941).

110. Pennekamp v. Florida, 328 U.S. 331 (1946).

111. Craig v. Harney, 334 U.S. 367 (1947).

112. 370 U.S. 375 (1962).

113. Professor Franklin sees the Court in the *Times* case as limiting *Beauharnais* to cases where a breach of peace actually is threatened; Franklin, *The Origins and Constitutionality of Limitations on Truth as a Defense in Tort Law,* 16 STAN.L.REV. 789, 820 (1964).

114. 343 U.S. 250, 263 n. 18 (1952).

115. 376 U.S. 254, 270 (1964).

II

116. Indeed, two further decisions have come down since April 8, 1964, the date of this lecture; see notes 152 and 157, *infra.*

117. See Note, *Private Attorneys General: Group Action in the Fight for Civil Liberties,* 58 YALE L.J. 575, 581–89 (1949); N.A.A.C.P. v. Button, 371 U.S. 415 (1963).

118. See discussion of Button case, *infra,* pp. 75–90.

119. See Bickel, *The Decade of School Desegregation: Progress and Prospects,* 64 COLUM.L.REV. 193 (1964).

120. 174 F.Supp. 351 (E.D.Ark. 1959).

121. 364 U.S. 479 (1960); see discussion, *infra,* pp. 99–105.

122. 174 F.Supp. 351, 354 (E.D.Ark. 1959).

123. American Communications Ass'n v. Douds, 339 U.S. 382 (1950); Garner v. Board of Public Works, 341 U.S. 716 (1951); Gerende v. Board of Supervisors, 341 U.S. 56 (1951); Adler v. Board of Education, 342 U.S. 485 (1952); Lerner v. Casey, 357 U.S. 468 (1958).

124. 344 U.S. 183 (1952).

125. 174 F.Supp. 351, 358 (E.D.Ark. 1959).

126. Perhaps the Court's use of *Weiman* as the key precedent in this context is simply evidence that *Weiman* truly involves a neutral principle.

127. 366 U.S. 293 (1961).

128. American Communications Ass'n v. Douds, 339 U.S. 482 (1950).

129. Gibson v. Florida Legislative Investigating Committee, 372 U.S. 539 (1963).

130. 371 U.S. 415 (1963).

131. 159 F.Supp. 503 (E.D.Va. 1958).

132. 360 U.S. 167 (1959).

133. *Id.* at 182.

134. 202 Va. 142 (1960).

135. Cf. Bickel, *op. cit., supra,* note 119; see Note, 73 YALE L.J. 90 (1963).

136. Cf. Bickel, *Applied Politics and the Science of Law,* in MENDELSON, FELIX FRANKFURTER: A TRIBUTE 164, 189 *et seq.* (1964).

137. 340 U.S. 290 (1951).

138. Krislov, *The Amicus Curiae Brief: From Friendship to Advocacy,* 72 YALE L.J. 694 (1963).

139. Lombard v. Louisiana, 373 U.S. 267 (1963).

140. These provisions appear to have survived in the law as finally enacted, July 2, 1964.

141. See Berger, *The New York State Law against Discrimination: Operation and Administration,* 35 CORNELL L.Q. 747 (1950).

142. *Op. cit., supra,* note 117.

143. 371 U.S. 415, 430–31, (1963).

144. *Id.* at 452–53.

145. Thornhill v. Alabama, 310 U.S. 88 (1940).

146. 371 U.S. 415, 433–34 (1963).

147. *Id.* at 436.

148. 357 U.S. 449 (1958).

149. 361 U.S. 516 (1960).

150. *Infra,* pp. 90 *et seq.*

151. 371 U.S. 415, 443–44 (1963).

152. In Brotherhood of Railroad Trainmen v. Virginia, 377 U.S. 1 (1964), decided April 20, 1964, after the date of this lecture, the Court, with Justice Harlan dissenting, approved on constitutional grounds a union solicitation plan and relied heavily on the Button case.

153. 278 U.S. 63 (1928).

154. *Supra,* note 148.

155. *Id.* at 462–63.

156. Sweezy v. New Hampshire, 354 U.S. 234 (1957).

157. This particular litigation was destined to have a complicated sequel in the Supreme Court. In the 1957 version of the case discussed in the text, the Court had passed only on the contempt aspect; it did not deal with the merits of the underlying ouster proceedings. The matter in one form or another came back to the Court three more times, climaxing in NAACP v. Alabama, 377 U.S. 288 (1964), decided on June 1. See also 360 U.S. 240 (1959), and 368 U.S. 16 (1961).

This most recent version of the case involves an appeal from the order of the Alabama courts permanently enjoining the NAACP from engaging in business in Alabama. The Supreme Court, speaking through Justice Harlan, reverses and remands the case back to the Alabama Supreme Court for the entry of a decree vacating the injunction and permitting the NAACP to take all steps necessary to qualify to do business in Alabama. The Court, with some reluctance, declines to formulate the decree itself. The Harlan opinion concludes with the following: "Should we unhappily be mistaken in our belief that the Supreme Court of Alabama

will promptly implement this disposition, leave is given the
association to apply to this court for further appropriate
relief."

Although not directly relevant to our main topic, the case
is interesting for us in two respects. First, Justice Harlan
is now the one who is exasperated with the performance of
a Southern court. It had been claimed that the state court's
decision rested on a non-federal ground, an Alabama rule
of appellate procedure. Justice Harlan rejects this claim as
"wholly unacceptable" and makes a careful review of the
Alabama precedents himself, stating: "Paying full respect
to the state court's opinion, it seems to us crystal clear that
the rule invoked by it cannot reasonably be deemed applicable
to this case."

Second, the very new precedent of the *New York Times*
case is cited. In weighing the alleged bases for the ouster
decree, the Court passes upon the claim that the NAACP had
"falsely charged" various Alabama officials with impro-
prieties. Justice Harlan finds this a constitutionally insufficient grounds for so direct an interference with freedom of
association as the ouster. It is, therefore, he says, not
necessary to speculate "on other possible constitutional in-
firmities to which these allegations may be subject, cf. *New
York Times* v. Sullivan. . . . "

For still other legal skirmishes of the NAACP, see NAACP
Committee on Offenses, 358 U.S. 40 (1958); NAACP v.
Bennett, 360 U.S. 471 (1959); NAACP v. Williams, 359 U.S.
550 (1959).

158. *Infra,* pp. 120–21.

159. *Supra,* note 149.

160. *Id.* at 528.

161. 366 U.S. 293 (1961). The other wing of this case
involving non-Communist affidavits as to officers of affiliated
organizations has been discussed separately, *supra,* pp. 74–75,
and see note 127.

162. 364 U.S. 497 (1960).

163. *Id.* at 485.

164. *Id.* at 488 *et seq;* see, for example, Lovell v. Griffin,
303 U.S. 444 (1937); Schneider v. State, 308 U.S. 147
(1939).

165. 341 U.S. 716 (1951).

166. *Supra,* note 120.

167. 364 U.S. 479, 499 (1960).

168. *Id.* at 496.

169. See the brilliant account in BOWER, ACTIONABLE DEFAMATION 332–35 (1908).

170. 364 U.S. 479, 494 (1960).

171. *Id.* at 495.

172. *Ibid.*

173. *Supra,* note 129.

174. See generally, TAYLOR, GRAND INQUEST (1955); BARTH, GOVERNMENT BY INVESTIGATION (1955); Kalven, *Mr. Alexander Meiklejohn and the Barenblatt Opinion,* 27 U.CHI.L.REV. 315 (1960).

175. 273 U.S. 135 (1927).

176. Watkins v. United States, 354 U.S. 178 (1957).

177. *Supra,* note 156.

178. Barenblatt v. United States, 360 U.S. 109 (1959).

179. Uphaus v. Wyman, 360 U.S. 72 (1959).

180. Wilkinson v. United States, 365 U.S. 399 (1961).

181. Braden v. United States, 365 U.S. 431 (1961).

182. Notably, Justice Clark in Josephson v. United States, 165 F.2d. 82 (CA 2 1947) and Justice Edgerton in Barsky v. United States, 167 F.2d. 241 (Dist.Ct.App. 1948).

183. See especially *Watkins, supra,* note 176.

184. See especially *Barenblatt, supra,* note 178.

185. 360 U.S. 109, 134 (1959).

186. 365 U.S. 399, 404 n. 5 (1961).

187. 365 U.S. 431, 456 (1961).

188. 360 U.S. 72, 79 (1959).

189. 372 U.S. 539, 582 (1963).

190. *Id.* at 546.

191. *Id.* at 557.

192. *Id.* at 580.

193. *Supra,* pp. 103–4, and note 169.

194. 372 U.S. 539, 559 (1963).

195. *Id.* at 561.

196. *Id.* at 573.

197. *Id.* at 572.

198. See Kalven & Steffen, *The Bar Admission Cases: An Unfinished Debate between Justice Harlan and Justice Black,* 21 LAW IN TRANSITION 155, 173–79 (1961).

199. Compare Talley v. California, 362 U.S. 60 (1960).

III

200. Once again, this third lecture was written prior to the most recent batch of sit-in cases; see *infra,* p. 161.

201. This was written in April, 1964. The point is that after "the long hot summer," it is still true.

202. For a classic statement of the law's conservatism with respect to self-help, see Kirby v. Foster, 17 R.I. 437, 22 Alt. 1111 (1891).

203. 368 U.S. 157 (1961).

204. This has been a tactic used only with extreme rarity by the Supreme Court; see Fiske v. Kansas, 274 U.S. 380 (1927); Thompson v. Louisville, 362 U.S. 199 (1960).

205. 109 U.S. 3 (1883).

206. See *supra,* note 200.

207. The Warren and Douglas opinions in *Garner* are, of course, worthy of full discussion in their own right; see Lewis, *The Sit-in Cases: Great Expectations,* [1963] Sup. Ct. Rev. 101.

208. 370 U.S. 154 (1962).

209. Shuttlesworth v. Birmingham, 373 U.S. 262 (1963).

210. Peterson v. Greenville, 373 U.S. 244 (1963).

211. Lombard v. Louisiana, 373 U.S. 267 (1963).

212. See *supra,* note 200.

213. Justice Harlan scrutinizes the facts as to consent very closely in *Garner,* 368 U.S. 157, 196–99 (1961), and concludes that the owner "did not want to risk losing Negro patronage in the store by requesting these petitioners to leave." In two of the three cases combined in *Garner,* therefore, he finds "implied consent."

214. 368 U.S. 157, 201–2 (1961).

215. 310 U.S. 296 (1940).

216. 368 U.S. 157, 203 (1961).

217. 310 U.S. 88 (1940).

218. 354 U.S. 284 (1957).

219. *Id.* at 297.

220. For a forceful and delightfully exasperated view of the picketing–free-speech analogy, see GREGORY, LABOR AND THE LAW, 334–50 (1946).

221. *Supra,* note 144.

222. 167 U.S. 43 (1897).

223. 307 U.S. 496 (1939).

224. 162 Mass. 510, 511, 39 N.E. 113 (1895).

225. 167 U.S. 43, 48 (1897).

226. 307 U.S. 496, 515 (1939).

227. 312 U.S. 569 (1941).

228. MEIKLEJOHN, POLITICAL FREEDOM 24–28 (1960).

229. 340 U.S. 315 (1951).

230. 340 U. S. 290 (1951).

231. The concurring opinion of Justice Frankfurter contains an elaborate and helpful summary of this entire line of precedent, 340 U.S. 268, 273 (1951).

232. 315 U.S. 568 (1942).

233. Hague v. C.I.O., 307 U.S. 496, 516 (1939).

234. 340 U.S. 268, 289 (1951).

235. 372 U.S. 229 (1963).

236. *Id.* at 229–31.

237. *Id.* at 235.

238. *Id.* at 237.

239. Compare Prosser, *Business Visitors and Invitees,* 26 MINN.L.REV. 573 (1942), where the author argues that the tort law on occupier liability has fallen into error in not preserving an old distinction based on the *public* nature of the place rather than, as today, on the specific invitation. Certain places were simply "open to the public."

240. 319 U.S. 141 (1942).

241. *Id.* at 146.

242. *Id.* at 148.

243. *Id.* at 157.

244. 326 U.S. 501 (1946).

245. *Id.* at 510. Justice Frankfurter adds a dictum which is congenial to the basic thesis being put forward in this lecture: "The technical distinctions on which a finding of 'trespass' so often depends are too tenuous to control decision regarding the scope of the vital liberties guaranteed by the Constitution."—*Id.* at 511.

246. *Id.* at 505.

247. *Id.* at 508–9.

248. *Id.* at 512.

249. *Id.* at 516.

250. See Tefft, *Marsh v. Alabama—A Suggestion Concerning Restrictive Covenants,* 4 NAT'L B.J. (1946); Justice Black dissenting in Bell v. Maryland, 378 U.S. 226, 318 (1964).

251. 297 N.Y. 339, 79 N.E.2d 433 (1948), *cert. denied,* 335 U.S. 886 (1948).

252. *Id.* at 348, and 436.

253. *Ibid.*

254. Saia v. New York, 334 U.S. 558 (1948).

255. Kovacs v. Cooper, 336 U.S. 77 (1949).

256. *Id.* at 86.

257. *Id.* at 86–87.

258. 343 U.S. 451 (1952).

259. Justice Frankfurter did not participate in the case, because his "feelings were so strongly engaged as a victim of the practice in controversy that I had better not participate in judicial judgment upon it."—*Id.* at 467.

260. *Id.* at 466.

261. *Id.* at 469.

262. *Ibid.* (Italics added.)

IV

263. In two the Court grants *certiorari,* Hamm v. City of Rock Hill, 377 U.S. 299 (1964), and Lupper v. Arkansas, 377 U.S. 989 (1964) ; in another, *certiorari* is denied, Ford v. Tennessee, 377 U.S. 994 (1964).

Five are remanded for further consideration in light of the current decisions, Drews v. Maryland, 377 U.S. 547 (1964) ; Williams v. North Carolina, 377 U.S. 548 (1964) ; Fox v. North Carolina, 377 U.S. 587 (1964) ; Green v. Virginia, 377 U.S. 550 (1964) ; Harris v. Virginia, 377 U.S. 552 (1964).

And in Mitchell v. City of Charleston, 377 U.S. 551 (1964), the Court reverses *per curiam* on the basis of the Bouie case.

264. For earlier discussion see Lewis, *The Sit-in Cases: Great Expectations,* [1963] Sup.Ct.Rev. 101; for discussions of the current sit-in cases, see Kurland, *Foreword: The Supreme Court 1963 Term,* 78 Harv.L.Rev. 143, 158–62 (1964) ; Paulsen, *The Sit-in Cases of 1964: "But Answer Came There None,"* [1964] Sup.Ct.Rev. 137.

265. The Civil Rights Act was enacted July 2, 1964. Title II covers public accommodations and prohibits refusal of entry and service on the basis of race. Hence, the federal legislation covers a considerable part, if not all, of the grievances against which the sit-in was designed to protest. This particular self-help measure may no longer be needed, since now the Negro under the Act has a legal right to enter. It is not yet established just what the scope of federal power under the Act is. Insofar as it is predicated on the commerce clause there will be some places of public accommodation to which the Act will not apply. Insofar as the Act is predicated on Section 5 of the Fourteenth Amendment, the situation is

less clear and appears to depend on what the Court will do with the Civil Rights Cases of 1883. As noted in the text, there is language in the Black dissent in the *Bell* case suggestive of a favorable view of congressional legislation under the Fourteenth Amendment; see Kurland, *op. cit., supra,* note 264, at 162. Finally, there is a useful appendix to the Douglas opinion in *Bell,* listing the states and cities which now have public accommodations laws. The universe of the sit-in is happily shrinking.

266. See note 203, *supra.*

267. See note 209, *supra.*

268. See note 210, *supra.*

269. See note 211, *supra.* In addition, there is the slight variant presented in Taylor v. Louisiana, 370 U.S. 154 (1962).

270. 378 U.S. 146 (1964).

271. A second aspect of the Barr cases involved criminal trespass and was disposed of *per curiam* on the basis of *Bouie* with Black, Harlan, and White dissenting.

272. 378 U.S. 153 (1964).

273. The Robinson case, alone of the five, involved a statute which unequivocally made remaining on property after a request to leave a criminal trespass.

274. The health regulation literally required not segregation of eating accommodations but "separate toilet and lavatory rooms." The property in question was a department store which catered to Negro customers in all other departments except the restaurant. The Court, although acknowledging that there is some strain in finding direct state action here, says: "The state through its regulations has become involved to such significant extent in bringing about restaurant segregation that the appellants' trespass convictions must be held to reflect state policy and, therefore, to violate the Fourteenth Amendment."

275. 378 U.S. 130 (1964).

276. On this point, compare Kurland, *op. cit., supra,* note 264, at 162: "It would be helpful if these and other similar cases would be labeled 'good for use in sit-in cases only.' "

277. Accordingly, the dissent would proceed to the constitutional question and decide it in favor of the convictions as they do in Bell v. Maryland.

278. 378 U.S. 347 (1964).

279. The Court is divided into three factions as in *Bell.* Justice Brennan is joined in his opinion by Justices Clark and Stewart. Justice Black is joined in his dissent by Justices Harlan and White. The Chief Justice and Justice Goldberg join in the opinion but would also reach the constitutional issue; Justice Douglas concurs in the result but would reach the constitutional issue.

280. 378 U.S. 226 (1964).

281. Prosser, Torts 62–63, 106 *et seq.* (1955). It appears, however, that the tort law, too, had its difficulties with the case of consent terminated after entry.

282. The majority may have somewhat the better of this corner of the dispute. First, the dissent is not making its point cleanly. The reason the defendants were not in fact "misled" was not because of clues from the statute that it covered the case of consent terminated after entry but because they knew their original entry into the luncheon sector was without consent. Yet it was precisely on the ambiguity of the non-consent in this context that Justice Harlan based his concurring opinion in *Garner;* see *supra,* note 213. Further, the majority seems correct that the failure of a statute to give fair warning that conduct is criminal is be judged objectively and not subjectively; compare the kind of vicarious championing of a good point that is permitted to the wretched defendant in Kunz v. New York, 340 U.S. 290 (1951).

283. Justice Goldberg, with whom the Chief Justice joins, indicates that he would have been content not to reach it, had not the dissent insisted on stating their views.

284. Compare Kalven and Steffen, *op. cit., supra,* note 198.

285. See *supra,* note 136.

286. Compare the dissent of Justice Jackson in Eisler v. United States, 338 U.S. 189, 196 (1948), a congressional contempt case. Eisler had fled the United States while the appeal was pending and the Court held the case moot. Jackson

protested: "Decision at this time is not urged as a favor to
Eisler. If only his interests were involved, they might well
be forfeited by his flight. But it is due to Congress and to
future witnesses before its committees that we hand down
a final decision. I therefore dissent from an expedient that
lends added credence to Eisler's petition, which I think is
without legal merit. I do not think we can run away from
the case just because Eisler has.

"I should not want to be understood as approving the
use that the Committee on Un-American Activities has frequently made of its power. But I think it would be an unwarranted act of judicial usurpation to strip Congress of
its investigatory power, or to assume for the courts the
function of supervising congressional committees. I should
affirm the judgment below and leave the responsibility for
the behavior of its committees squarely on the shoulders of
Congress."

287. The mood of the dissent is reflected in the full
sentence: "Nor does the principle properly understood and
applied impose a rigid, arbitrary, and inexorable command
that courts should never decide a constitutional question in
any single case if subtle ingenuity can think up any conceivable technique that might, if utilized, offer a distant
possibility of avoiding decision."

288. 334 U.S. 1 (1948).

289. *Supra,* note 203.

290. *Supra,* note 211.

291. "The Congress shall have power to enforce, by
appropriate legislation, the provisions of this article."

292. 109 U.S. 27 (1883).

293. *Supra,* p. 132.

DATE DUE
